HENRIK WERGELAND

POEMS

"My dearest dream is for internationality of poems and poets, binding the lands of the earth closer than all treaties and diplomacy."

Walt Whitman.

HENRIK WERGELAND

POEMS

TRANSLATED BY
G. M. GATHORNE-HARDY, JETHRO BITHELL
AND I. GRØNDAHL

WITH AN INTRODUCTION BY
G. M. GATHORNE-HARDY

AND A PREFACE BY
FRANCIS BULL
PROFESSOR OF SCANDINAVIAN LITERATURE
IN THE UNIVERSITY OF OSLO

GREENWOOD PRESS, PUBLISHERS
WESTPORT, CONNECTICUT

Originally published in 1929
by Gyldendal Norsk Forlag, Oslo
and Hodder & Stoughton, Ltd., London

First Greenwood Reprinting 1970

Library of Congress Catalogue Card Number 74-98798

SBN 8371-3159-6

Printed in United States of America

CONTENTS

PREFACE

In the eyes of Norwegians Henrik Wergeland's name has a more radiant nimbus than any other name in the history of our literature. Not that we consider him to be greater than Holberg, Ibsen or Bjørnson—to mention only the most famous among our authors. But Wergeland seems to be personally nearer to us; as it were, a dearer friend. Outside Norway it has not always been easy to understand this feeling. It has been suggested that the admiration of his countrymen was due to national over-estimation of his merits and regret at his early death, rather than to the intrinsic value of his work.

We cannot expect others than his fellow countrymen to be interested in Wergeland's complete works, which, in the new edition at present appearing, will comprise more than twenty large volumes.[1] It may be said without fear of exaggeration, that at least four-fifths of his writings are of interest only to those who wish to study the history of Norway and the personality of Henrik Wergeland himself. But the remainder, above all the collection of lyrical poems, will, I am profoundly convinced, afford unforgettable delight to every lover of poetry.

Up to the present, however, these poems have not been very accessible to readers unacquainted with our

[1] Ed. by Herman Jæger and D. A. Seip, Steenske Forlag, Oslo.

language. Not many of Wergeland's poems have been translated, and a foreigner learning Norwegian must work hard and long before he can successfully cope with Wergeland. Indeed, few of our writers are more difficult to follow. Though neither vague nor obscure, he is certainly involved and intricate—his images succeed each other in such number and with such rapidity, that the ordinary mortal is left breathless. This almost Shakespearian exuberance of imagery is especially characteristic of Wergeland's juvenile poetry; and even in the translations which follow, some of the early poems may seem difficult. The reader will probably do well to begin with the later poems until he has familiarized himself with the qualities of Wergeland's verse.

If one had to distinguish between earthly and heavenly poets, one would unhesitatingly place Henrik Wergeland among the latter; or, perhaps, to borrow a phrase of his own coining, among the "poetic poets". With flowers and butterflies, with a tree or a rabbit, he talks as if he were one of themselves, and he is in his element in the fairyland of the clouds or among the stars of the Milky Way. But men and women and everyday realities he cannot quite understand. For the miserable, destitute and outcast his heart yearns, and he is consumed with a passionate love of his people and mankind; but the human figures in his poetic works are apt to become types and mouthpieces for his ideas, rather than actual persons. The only portrait he has painted to the life is his own. But his self-portrait reveals such a rich and striking personality, that it fascinates every one who becomes acquainted with it.

Henrik Wergeland once said that he could climb to Heaven on a gossamer, and his readers will admit the truth of his words. His poetry starts on earth, but it rises straight to the skies. Reality cannot hold him, he soon soars to the freer realm of ideas. He does not depend upon concrete instances to symbolize his thoughts; the idea emerges directly in the poem, though it is always richly clad in imagery, decked with "lyrical ivy". And his imagery is not sculptured in the calm beauty of classical form, but created by visual fancy charged with feeling. Every picture is painted with such warmth and intensity that it moves the heart as much as it pleases the inward eye. With a poet's intuition Bjørnstjerne Bjørnson saw that Henrik Wergeland's leading characteristic was "the amplitude of mind in which ideas are deepened and intensified" *("den sindsfylde hvori forestillingerne inderliggjøres").*

Henrik Wergeland was not without philosophical power and insight; but his poetry is distinguished, above all, by the spontaneous originality of his genius. He responds immediately to every impression; his poems are not the fruit of meditation, they are conceived and born in a moment, under stress and strain. His feelings are as violent as a child's, his thoughts and visions turn into myths, as they do in the minds of primitive people. Directness rather than polish being the chief quality of his verse, he appeals to our simple feelings, to the child in us. A title his father once suggested for his first collection of poems—"Harp-notes of Friend-

ship, Love, Freedom and Country"—would embrace
the principal subjects of Henrik Wergeland's poetry;
but the harper's chords should not be beautiful sens-
uous sounds only, they should inspire the hearers to
translate feeling into action and life. Henrik Wergeland
himself sang, lived, and died in accordance with his
feelings and convictions, and true to his strong philan-
thropic impulse. There are hundreds of examples on
record of his impulsiveness and his primitive reaction
to the world around him, which involved him in trouble
and betrayed him into ill-considered acts. But, for all
that, he could honestly claim on his death-bed that
he had kept the promise given in his youth, and used
all his powers in the service of his countrymen and
humanity. Thus his short, but full life furnished an
eloquent commentary on his poetry.

Nils Collett Vogt describes him in words which may
be rendered somewhat as follows:

"Seraph-like, yet earth-loving,
Inebriate, yet sober;
the sunshine of his thought
bathing images in flood.
And yet at whiles the tumult
was stilled to song that glided
like a stream flower-fringed.
He was tender as childhood.

A storm sweeping over Norway,
to shatter or to harden;
a heaven open as springtime,
heaven-wide his embrace.

> Dead things spake at his bidding,
> while here he walked among us;
> the very stones had souls then,
> bestowed by his grace."

Mr. Gathorne-Hardy's introduction contains a short biography of the poet, which admirably leads up to his works, and the selection of translations which follows seems to me to have been made with great care and understanding. It is varied and representative, and gives samples of Wergeland's art at its best. Of the renderings into English it is not for me to speak— the British public must judge of them; but I cherish the hope and belief that they will convince the reader that Henrik Wergeland was something more than a local Norwegian singer, that, in fact, his place is among the great poets who have created values for all peoples and all times.

Francis Bull.

INTRODUCTION

The name of Henrik Wergeland is a household word wherever the Norwegian language is understood, or its literature studied: in his native country, great as was his reputation at the time of his death, it is safe to say that it has grown with the passage of time, and that few critics would now be found there who would dispute his eminence as a figure in modern Norwegian literature. His importance is admitted even by those to whose individual tastes he does not appeal. "Who is he, really," writes Erik Vullum, "this Henrik Wergeland, under whose silent sovereignty we live? He has become for us what the domestic idol was for our forefathers. The god might be hated or loved. No matter. All had to worship him and pay him tribute; all had to have him with them in their labours." This testimony is confirmed and enhanced by still more distinguished voices. Bjørnson, after a reference to a number of Wergeland's best-known poems, declared that "if a foreigner well versed in world-literature could read these and other works of Henrik Wergeland, he would unconditionally place him among the greatest of his contemporaries, and in what was peculiar to him—for every poet has his speciality—would regard him as unsurpassed." Among living poets of Norway, Nils Collett Vogt and Olaf Bull have both paid graceful tribute to Wergeland's genius, the former comparing him in his great national cantata to the sun, cleaving a furrow in the darkness of his country's cultural history and bringing in the day. It is true that Ibsen, who was morbidly sensitive to any suggestion of an influence in his work external to himself, does not join in this chorus of appreciation. Almost the only reference to Wergeland which I can trace in his writings is a passage which couples a loan from the older poet's ideas with a slighting allusion to "Poet Pedersen".[1] Yet it is impossible for anyone who studies the work of both writers to resist the conclusion that Ibsen was materially influenced by the poetry of his predecessor. A story is told how, on the occasion of an unexpected visit, Ibsen was seen hastily thrusting under a cushion a book which turned out to be a volume of Wergeland, and, however apocryphal this anecdote may be, it is impossible to read, for example, the finale of Wergeland's poem, "Spaniolen", and the last act of Ibsen's "Brand", without perceiving a resemblance too close to be explained as coincidence. "Brand", indeed, is full of reminiscences of Wergeland; the "be thyself" of "Efter Tidens Leilighed" (see p. 85) is almost the keynote both of this drama and its com-

---

[1] (Love) is a dandelion, thriving best
When by man's heel or horse's hoof 'tis pressed;
Yes, sprouting shoots for every leaf you tread,
As poet Pedersen has finely said.

                              Kjærlighedens Komedie.

  Cf. Den Første Gang, p. 53. With Ibsen's allusion Mr .Grøndahl suggests contrasting a further quotation from Nils Collett Vogt:
"Be greeted! From out of my heart be thou greeted,
Thou spring-flower bringing my youth and his name
Who was both the lark and spring-torrent in Norway,
Who ever bore wings, and who never was tame!"

panion, "Peer Gynt", while Brand's appeal to his con-
gregation to be both men and priests, and to make a
temple of the land, is a close paraphrase of the conclus-
ion of Wergeland's "Mennesket", where everyone be-
comes "a King to the earth and a priest to God."

In the work of Bjørnstjerne Bjørnson, the other out-
standing figure in modern Norwegian literature, the
influence is not only continually recognisable, but would
have been freely acknowledged. Bjørnson, the many-
sided poet politician, played in fact, in the latter half
of the nineteenth century, a part corresponding most
remarkably to that which Wergeland acted in the years
immediately preceding it. Both on his own merits, and
by reason of the influence which his work exerted upon
his successors, Henrik Wergeland is in fact a poet whom
no student of the modern literature of Norway can afford
lightly to pass over, while he may also have significance
for the present generation.

Wergeland is not merely a leading figure in the national
literature of his own country. He is this, but he is more.
While it is true that he consecrated the energies of a
peculiarly active life to the service of his own country,
his work is uniquely distinguished from that of any of
his compatriots by the affinities which it shows with the
spirit which, in his youth, was creating a new movement
in literature throughout the whole of Europe. To say
this is not to question his originality. As Shelley has
asserted, "there must be a resemblance, which does not
depend upon their own will, between all the writers of
any particular age. They cannot escape from subjection
to a common influence which arises out of an infinite

combination of circumstances belonging to the times in which they live, though each is in a degree the author of the very influence by which his being is thus pervaded." One may go further, and claim that the wider are the sympathies, and the more sensitive to impressions the nature of the poet, the less isolated will he stand with regard to the spirit of his age. There is a paradox and an irony about the fact that Henrik Wergeland should have established a reputation for an exclusive nationalism among contemporary admirers and opponents alike, when in fact, of all Norwegian writers, he owed least to purely Scandinavian models, and was of all of them the most cosmopolitan in his interests and his disposition.

Without entering at this stage more closely into the question of Wergeland's relationship to his literary contemporaries, and his reaction to the common inspiration of his age, it may be pointed out here that the young poet grew up under a conjunction of influences calculated, to an exceptional degree, to feed his natural genius with the necessary inspiration. From these contemporary circumstances he derived more than from the remoter origins of his family. His name is a Danicized corruption from Verkland, a farm in the Sogn district of western Norway, with which, however, the poet's ancestors had severed their connection as early as 1747. Henrik retained sufficient interest in his origin to allude to it in a passage in "The English Pilot" included among the selections in this volume (p. 140):—

> "from Sognefylke's sheer
> Sea-encompassed savage crests,
> Through those hardy warrior breasts,

Flowed the fervent strains of blood
To my own ancestral line."

It was, however, in the town of Kristiansand, in the
extreme south of Norway, that Henrik Arnold Werge-
land was born, on June 17, 1808. At the time of his
birth, poetry was newly entering upon the great renais-
sance already referred to, asserting all over Europe its
emancipation from the fetters of pseudo-classical con-
vention which had hampered it during the preceding
age. This movement coincided with, and was to a great
extent inspired by, the great awakening of the desire
for political liberty which was inaugurated by the French
Revolution a few years before Wergeland's birth, and
which was destined in the near future to stimulate wide-
spread and ultimately succesful struggles for national
independence. In this movement, both in its nationalist
aspect and in its aspiration towards a democratic ideal,
Norway was among the first countries to achieve success.
In 1814, when the poet was but six years old, his nation
emerged from about four centuries of virtual subordina-
tion to Denmark, and, though destined for nearly another
hundred years to be connected with Sweden by a personal
union under the same sovereign, she entered upon this
connection as an independent people, ruled under a con-
stitution framed—in an extremely democratic spirit—by
elected representatives of her own at the epoch-making
assembly of Eidsvoll. At this assembly, one of the most
prominent figures was the poet's father, Nicolai Werge-
land, a pastor of the established Lutheran church, who
at the time of Henrik's birth was a teacher in the gram-
mar school of Kristiansand. In 1817, however, he was

appointed to the living of Eidsvoll, and it was accordingly on this spot, with all its inspiring national associations, in daily intercourse with one of those who had contributed to its historical importance, that the boy's most impressionable years were destined to be spent. Apart from his association with the achievement of Norwegian independence, Nicolai Wergeland exerted a formative influence upon his son's development which was of cardinal importance. He was a man of remarkably wide culture and broad views, particularly interested in the English literature of his time, a subscriber to the "Edinburgh Review", and a warm admirer of Byron. His English tastes are remarked on by Latham in his book "Norway and the Norwegians" (2 vols, 1840): even the piano and the carpet at Eidsvoll rectory came, we are told, from our country. Nicolai was, however, also a keen disciple of Rousseau, under the influence of whom he drew up, in the year of his son's birth, a systematic scheme of education divided into 43 rules. Fortunately, the general spirit of the system was of a nature to allow the child to follow his natural bent, and develop in almost complete freedom. In his religious views, the pastor leaned towards the prevailing rationalism of his time, and consequently regarded the general enlightenment of his parishioners as the principal duty of his calling—a view which his son inherited—while the rather arid negations of his creed left a spiritual void which gave room for Henrik's poetic pantheism.

Politically, Nicolai was associated at Eidsvoll with the unpopular party which had advocated from the first a union with Sweden, a fact which may to some extent explain the apparent inconsistency of his son's devotion to King Carl Johan (Bernadotte). His attitude towards Denmark, however, was one of uncompromising hostility, and he was known as the author of a pamphlet upon "Denmark's political Crimes against Norway". It was, in fact, from his father more than anyone else that the young Henrik derived his pronouncedly anti-Danish opinions. Though undistinguished as a poet, Nicolai was a sound critic, and was not without artistic accomplishments; he was an amateur painter of unusual talent, and an enthusiastic musician, while his prose writings fully deserve to be classed as literature.

The poet's mother, while her intellectual influence was comparatively small, was in her young days an amateur actress with a considerable local reputation, and came of an artistic family, the Thaulows, Danish in origin but settled for many generations in Norway. Her mother was Scottish. The qualities which Henrik seems to have derived from his mother were rather those of the heart than the head, an affectionate and sympathetic nature, the impetuous generosity of which was in marked contrast to Nicolai's rather calculating and far-sighted character. Of the remaining members of the family, none are of special importance with the exception of a sister, Camilla, born in 1813, who attained considerable distinction as a novelist and prose writer, as well as in the movement for women's rights in Norway. A book of hers, entitled "I de lange Nætter" (In the long nights), is a leading source of information on her brother's earlier days.

In view of an erroneous idea which I have found somewhat widely prevalent on the subject of Wergeland's health, it seems advisable to emphasize the robust open-air life which he led. The notion that he suffered from a weak constitution and indifferent health is doubtless due to the extent to which attention has been concentrated on the output of the last year of his life. That he died young was due rather to his characteristic recklessness than to any constitutional weakness. He grew up exceptionally tall and strong—short sight being his only serious physical defect. He was in the habit of constantly swimming in the river near his home at a time when it was still encumbered with floating ice, and he was an enthsiuastic ski-runner at a period when the use of skis was for the most part purely utilitarian and confined to the peasantry. He led, in fact, a pre-eminently out-door life, and his health throve by it.

At the age of 11, Henrik Wergeland went to school in the capital, where his favourite studies were botany and history, and where he almost immediately began to indulge a precocious talent for story writing. His first published work, a crude but not unpromising effort in the melodramatic style of romance then fashionable, was entitled "Blodstenen" (the Blood-stone), and appeared in the columns of "Morgenbladet" as early as 1821.

When he was 17, Wergeland left school for Kristiania University, where he began studying theology, with the intention of following his father's calling. The university students of this time, representative of the first generation to grow to manhood under the new constitution, played an active and naturally somewhat rowdy part in the public life of the capital. In these activities, the theological students, for some reason, seem to have been the most unruly; but though Wergeland claims, and is usually allowed, to have played a leading part, he certainly did not engage the attentions of the police so frequently as some of his associates. He acquired, however, a character for "levitas juvenilis" with the university authorities, which was destined seriously to prejudice his later career, and was rumoured to be addicted to heavy drinking. With this reputation the poet's own character of himself agrees, and some hints in Latham's account seem to confirm it, but when the truth of the matter came subsequently to be tested in a court of law, substantial evidence of intemperate habits proved to be almost completely lacking. The real truth of the matter seems to be that Wergeland, like many another young man, liked to make himself out more disreputable than he was:[1] he had, moreover, an excitable temperament and a disregard of convention which might easily give rise to misunderstandings. His worst enemy, Procurator Praëm, probably summed up the matter justly when he said,—"when Wergeland is excited, his uncontrolled behaviour may easily cause one who does not know him to believe him intoxicated, when this is not really the case."

It is evident, however, that his activities as a student soon began to make him conspicuous as well as popular among his contemporaries, and his literary talents now brought him into some request, as a satirist and song-writer. It was a stimulating time, for these were the

---

[1] Associating himself with Prince Hal:
  "I'll so offend, to make offence a skill;
  Redeeming time when men least think I will." I. G.

years during which the King made his most strenuous efforts to stop the observance of the 17th of May,— the anniversary of the Eidsvoll constitution. These attempts culminated in 1829 in the notorious "Torveslag", or Battle of the Market Place, when a number of unoffending citizens were charged by the cavalry. In this disturbance, young Wergeland, who seems to have been behaving at the time with perfect propriety, received a blow with the flat of a sabre from a passing soldier, whereupon he packed up the student uniform which had been thus insulted, and sent it with his compliments to the commandant, Baron Wedel Jarlsberg. The story of this characteristic action was of course soon all over the town, and increased its hero's notoriety. This was not, however, Wergeland's first clash with the military authorities. In the previous year, while visiting the camp at Gardermoen, on the occasion of a review, he had got into a dispute with a non-commissioned officer, named Lie, which led to charges and counter-charges, and an enquiry before a mixed civil and military commission, which dragged on for the amazing period of five years! As Lie's legal representative, there appeared the already mentioned Procurator Praëm, who began in this way a feud destined to last for the greater part of Wergeland's short life.

These disturbances, however, are far from constituting the whole history of Wergeland's career during his student days. Many of the poems of his early period were now first published, mainly in the columns of "Morgenbladet", including the memorial ode to his dead friend, Peter Krefting (p. 1), which is perhaps the earliest of his verses to display remarkable and highly original qualities, and is the first of a number of poems, examples of which will be found in the present volume, which are the poet's response to the friendship for which he craved, even though his disposition was certainly not of a kind to encourage or facilitate intimacy. The verses to Krefting appeared in 1827, the year which saw also the publication of "Ah!", the first of the farces written under the pseudonym, "Siful Sifadda", adopted by Wergeland when writing in a militantly satirical vein. "Siful Sifadda", the "twin brother who always comported himself bravely," was almost regarded by the poet as a separate personality, though he never made the slightest attempt to conceal his identity with the satirist. In the following year, 1828, appeared a very crude tragedy, "Sinclair's Death", and the farce, "Irreparabile Tempus", which contains some passages not unworthy of the poet's subsequent reputation. The following lines, in Mr. Grøndahl's translation, descriptive of different human attitudes towards life, may be given as a sample:—

> ". . . . . Now, some are lying still
> And sleeping all the time, rending the darkness
> Only with yawns—like to the sleeper saints—
> Till down the roof comes by itself, and they
> Must swallow half the final snore and come,
> Rubbing their stupid, blinking eyes, into
> The fresh air blowing just beyond the wall.
> They are the lazy ones. But others run
> About and madly scratch with tooth and claw
> The murky wall on every side, until
> It crumbles, cracks, and lets in the fierce sunshine
> That scorches them like withered grass: their force
> Was spent, instead of gradually growing."

But, in spite of the many attempts which Wergeland made to write drama, this was a branch of literature in which he was never really successful. He seems to have unwisely turned his attention in this direction through an enthusiasm for Shakespeare, whose works he had read in a Danish translation. Throughout his career, he continued to write plays of various kinds, but few were ever acted, and fewer still deserved production. Wergeland almost wholly lacked the dramatist's power of characterisation: true child of Nature as he was—"careful of the type and careless of the single life"—he was more interested in humanity in the mass than in its individual variations. It has been well said of him by Mr. Grøndahl that "to him mankind, a living, changing being, and part of a larger one, is more actually Man than the individual is." Therefore, although it seems likely that his poetic activity was generally stimulated by his introduction to Shakespeare, what is best in his work cannot be said to owe much to the influence of the English poet. His real genius first began to be apparent in 1829, the year when he finished his university course, and gave to the world the first collected volume of his poems, under the title, "Digte, første Ring."

These firstfruits of Wergeland's muse are generally inspired and largely pervaded by the composite female figure which the author names "Stella," and the whole period down to and including the publication of "Creation, Humanity and Messiah" marks a definite phase in Wergeland's literary development, which may be conveniently classified as the "Stella period." During these years, in fact, the young student was continuously in love with a bewildering succession of young women, who evinced a common reluctance to return his turbulent affections. Of these the most important were Hulda Malthe (1826—7), and Elise Wolff (1828): the attachment to the former, though short-lived, was sufficiently serious to lead to an attempt at suicide on the part of the rejected lover. But the composite figure of Stella is very largely idealized, and stands more for the young poet's reactions towards the eternal feminine than for any concrete object of his immature and unstable affactions. The love-poetry of the Stella period shows a marked contrast in this respect to that which he later on lavished upon his wife, and the principal importance of these earlier infatuations lies in the stimulus which they contributed, together with the political events of the time, to the ripening genius of the poet.

I confess that to me the advent of a new and strikingly impressive literary personality is even more evident in the poetry of "Digte, første Ring" than in the more restrained and mature verse of Wergeland's later development. For all its wild eccentricity and crude lack of taste, it is marked by a richness of imagery and an originality of form which makes it, though not the best, perhaps the most arresting work of Wergeland's whole career. The form may easily be taken, at a first glance, for formlessness, so great is the departure from the conventional models of the time; yet the metrical discipline is seen on a closer examination to be generally strict and severe, based apparently upon the rules of Latin prosody, though never conforming exactly to any actual classical model. These dactylic metres, employed for the most part in unrhymed verse, give a passionate swing to these poems which succeeds in expressing, to a very remarkable degree, the fiery eagerness of the young poet's character. Blemishes and absurdities are indeed both frequent and conspicuous, but they are manifestly due either to a youthful innocence which is incapable of distinguishing good from bad, or to the defects of qualities inherently poetic,—a turbulent imagination which presents ideas in so swift and fluent a sequence as to give no time for discrimination, and a passionate love of freedom which sets even the most salutary conventions at defiance. As Latham says, Wergeland at this stage of his career never seems to have rejected an idea, and it is evident, not only in these early works but throughout his life, that ideas and images raced one another in his fertile brain much faster than they could be written down, far less selected. Set a blank sheet of paper before him at any stage of his career, and it was at once covered with ideas expressed in verse. Such fatal fluency is not, of course, compatible with a faultless technique. The machine-gunner, however effective, can never claim so large a percentage of hits as the deliberate sniper. But in the midst of all this temperamental effervescence we can constantly discern the "disjecti membra poetae," and sometimes, as in the passage selected from his address to his little rabbit, (p. 5), he rises, even at this early stage, to heights which he never surpassed.

In this passage, his grasp of the idea of an evolutionary and continuous creation seems far in advance of his age, though something of the same conception may be traced

in the Prophetic Books of William Blake. This theme,
to which Wergeland frequently recurred, e.g. in the
opening words of his cantata, "Vord Lys!" (Let there
be Light, p. 76), is the connecting thread which runs
through his great dramatic epic, "Skabelsen, Mennesket
og Messias" (Creation, Humanity and Messiah), which,
composed with a really amazing swiftness, appeared in
1830, and has been well described by the Danish critic,
Schwanenflügel, as "a grand poetic overture to the July
Revolution." In the conception of a gradual advance
towards human perfection, which is embodied in this
work, he owes perhaps some debt to the Norwegian
philosopher, Niels Treschow, though we know that in
his earlier poem, "Napoleon," he had arrived indepen-
dently at some of Treschow's conclusions, before he had
ever studied his works. Treschow was an early exponent
of the evolutionary theory, though he traced mankind
from an amphibian rather than a simian ancestry, our
first parent being, as Latham quaintly expresses it, not
an ape but a walrus! Treschow's influence upon Werge-
land was, in fact, rather confirmatory than educational;
placing the seal of scientific philosophy upon ideas due
in the first instance to poetic intuition. An influence
more directly traceable in "Skabelsen, Mennesket og
Messias," and even in the revised version, "Mennesket,"
which Wergeland brought out immediately before his
death, is that of Byron. The spirit character, Phun-
Abiriel, a compound of intellectual scepticism and
energetic action, is a typically Byronic figure, though
the sympathies of Wergeland are clearly opposed to the
doubts expressed by this being. The style as well as the

thought of the poem shows marked Byronic influences; this becomes very evident on comparing it with passages in "Cain" and "Heaven and Earth"—e.g. Scene III of the latter. In fact, Wergeland would hardly have denied these resemblances: originally he intended to borrow for his poem the title, "Heaven and Earth," and though he succeeded in ridding himself, at a comparatively early stage, from the incubus of doubt with which his study of the English poet had afflicted him, he still retained an admiration for Byron's genius sufficient to lead him, rather extravagantly, to couple his name with that of Plato in the verses "Til en Gran". (See p. 34). The allusion in the poem, "Paa Havet i Storm," (At Sea in a Storm), describing a spiritual experience of the year 1831,—

Farewell! Fly to the forest again,
Thou Byron's vulture, that hidest, too foul to be seen,
Thy ravening head in my heart . . .

should not be interpreted as referring to Byron himself, for whom Wergeland's admiration evidently still continued, but to the torturing doubts which had assailed the British poet, and whose gnawings Wergeland himself had for a time experienced. Yet the Norwegian's imperfect knowledge of the English language protected him from any lasting temptation to imitate the style of Byron, once he had definitely shaken off the spell of his ideas.

The existence of other influences is more open to question. In spite of Wergeland's expressed admiration for Shakespeare, we must remember that it was Shakespeare at second hand, in a Danish translation, who could indeed divert his energy to unwise attempts at drama,

but could hardly affect his literary style.[1] For Henrik
Steffens, the Germanicized Norwegian romantic who
certainly inspired the Danish poet, Oehlenschläger,
Wergeland no doubt felt an intellectual sympathy, as
is shown in the dedication of "Skabelsen, Mennesket
og Messias." Some of Steffens' work shows affinities
with the pantheistic views expressed by Wergeland, but,
as will be made clear later, Wergeland definitely rejected
the backward-looking romanticism for which Steffens
stood, after one very early and never repeated experiment.

It was in fact Wergeland's marked originality which
exposed him at this stage, with "Digte første Ring"
and "Skabelsen" to his credit, to the hostile criticism
of a rival, and more conventional, school of thought.
In August of 1831, the attack was opened by the publi-
cation of an anonymous poem in the columns of Morgen-
bladet:—

TO HENRIK WERGELAND

How long will you indulge in senseless raving,
In crazy brandishing of Quixote's spear?
See how, for all your airy wings a-waving,
Straight for a bottomless morass you steer!
The sun you seek is wildfire of the bog,
A crawling eft the Pegasus you flog!

Then murmur not that none of us is able
To judge a genius soaring past our sight:
Where is the art in cutting reason's cable
To drift about in realms of cloudy night?
Your place assured a thousand votes will fix,
The place the Muse reserves for—lunatics.

[1] The sympathetic influence of Shakespeare's imagination
on Wergeland is shown by Trygve Tonstad, in the quarterly
"Edda," Oslo 1929. I. G.

Such imputation of insanity seems to be the stock criticism of any poet who breaks new ground. We recall the review of Shelley's work as "drivelling prose run mad," or Byron's description of Wordsworth in "English Bards and Scotch Reviewers,"—

> Convincing all, by demonstration plain,
> Poetic souls delight in prose insane;
> . . . all who view the "idiot in his glory,"
> Conceive the bard the hero of the story.

The author of the verses in Morgenbladet was soon revealed as Johan Sebastian Welhaven, himself a poet of very considerable talent, whose intervention in the controversy was lent as added piquancy by the fact that he was the object of the affections of his opponent's sister, Camilla, and indeed appeared for a time, and up to a point, to reciprocate her feelings. Thus began a literary feud which separated cultured Norway for some years into two opposing camps. Welhaven followed up his verses with an effective and amusing, though unfair and one-sided review of Wergeland's claims as a poet, which was answered, no less effectively and with far more balance, by the poet's father, Nicolai.[1]

The nature of this controversy is often completely misunderstood, and it is, indeed, doubtful whether the real issue was even grasped by the protagonists. It is usual to state that Wergeland represented the crude nationalistic standpoint; Welhaven the more cultured cosmopolitan. It would be almost more correct to assert

---

[1] Both Henrik and Nicolai Wergeland referred to Shakespeare in their fight against the dogmatic estheticism of the time, much as Lessing had previously done in Germany.

the exact opposite. It is true that Wergeland regarded himself, and was regarded, as above all else a national poet and prophet, and that he rejected the canons of criticism which his antagonist imported from Denmark. But in relying upon Denmark, through which literary fashions penetrated but slowly, Welhaven only succeeded in keeping steadily behind the times. Wergeland's nationalism, on the other hand, was tempered by an interest in contemporary movements, literary and political, which was really cosmopolitan, and he consequently takes his place naturally in the great poetic revolution or renaissance of his age. The issue between the poet and his critic was therefore, in reality, merely a phase of the dispute which we can trace about this time all over Europe and the British Isles, between the advocates of a cramping formalism and the apostles of a new freedom—between the ideas of versification as craftsmanship and poetry as the vehicle of a quasi-religious message and as a political force.

For the revolution which affected poetry towards the end of the eighteenth and the beginning of the nineteenth century had as its key-note liberty. The label, romanticism, which is commonly attached to it, is deplorably inadequate. The mediaevalism which characterises much of the literature of this time, and to which the term "romanticism' might properly be applied, was but an occasional by-product of the forces at work. In part it was the result of political nationalism, which awakened an interest in the past glories of the race, in part it was a purely literary movement, the stages of which were —(1.) anti-classicism, (2.) an admiration for folk-poetry and ballads, fostered by the vogue of such works as Percy's "Reliques" and Macpherson's "Ossian." The latter in particular exerted a tremendous influence all over the continent. But of that branch of the new school which sought inspiration in the past, Wergeland was emphatically not a disciple. The one experiment in this genre which he made at the very outset of his literary carceer—"Sigmund Brestesons Saga"—was abandoned before completion, and the merest fragment, in the revised form which it takes in the poem "Et gammel-norskt Herresæde" (see p. 39) was all that was per-manently preserved. In his advice "to a young poet" (p. 31), Wergeland explicitly repudiates a school whose "antiquarian ants" are enthused by the dust of "grave-mounds hiding barbarian days", and this attitude he thenceforward steadily maintained. The opening words of this poem are in fact a direct challange, word by word, to the creed proclaimed by his Danish contemporary, Oehlenschläger, in his well-known poem, "Guldhornene."[1] The new liberty which was being claimed for the poet gave, as Wergeland saw, plenty of scope for an inspira-tion derived from more practical matters. In its aspira-tion towards freedom from the tyranny of rules which

[1]

OEHLENSCHLÄGER	WERGELAND
De higer og søger	Skjald, ei se du tilbage
I gamle bøger,	Ei mod den *runede steen*
I oplukte *høie*	Ei imod *højen,* der gjemmer
Med speidende øie,	barbariske dage!
Paa sværd og *skjolde*	Lad ligge de *skjolde!* lad *smuldre*
I muldne volde,	de *been!*
Paa *runestene*	
Blandt *smuldnede bene.*	

fettered the verse of the preceding age, it found and
felt a common ground with the political and religious
movements of the same period. Reaction against a
cramping authoritarianism was, in fact, in the air, and
all aspects of life were affected by it. Until the advent
of Wergeland, poetry—so-called—had been in Norway
a genteel accomplishment for comfortably placed officials
to practise in their spare time. In his hands, and in those
of men similarly inspired all over Europe, it became the
articulate expression of the whole spirit of the age, a
force potent for the direction of national destinies and
the aspirations of mankind. The fundamental incom-
patibility of the temperaments of Wergeland and Wel-
haven was materially aggravated by the circumstances
of contemporary Norway. The fact that the country
was making a fresh start, struggling with economic
difficulties and lack of cultural training, affected the
two poets in characteristically different ways. In a
garden in winter, one man will see the ugliness of the
bare earth, while another is preoccupied with the prospects
of future growth and seeks to interest himself in its
development. Or, on a building site, one is offended by
the apparent desolation and the raw heaps of new brick,
while another grows enthusiastic over the progress which
he visualises, and in which he endeavours to play an
active part. All the crudity which Welhaven saw filled
him with repulsion, and drove him back upon himself:
but, while his aesthetic soul shivered at the dissonances
around him, his rival was busy playing his environment
into harmony with himself. There was, indeed, much
justification for either point of view, but there can be

no doubt as to which was of the greater service in the cultural development of the nation.

I find myself quite unable to agree with the late Sir Edmund Gosse, who, in "the Oxford Book of Scandinavian Verse," states that Wergeland "laid the strictures of Welhaven to heart." Certainly it is not true that, as the same author asserts, "he himself refrained from counter-attack." On the contrary, the two poets were engaged for some time in a constant exchange of satirical rhymes, and Camilla, in her diary, records one occasion in which she aroused her brother's violent anger by erasing from his manuscript some personal remarks directed against his opponent. It was quite natural that, as he grew older, Wergeland should have purged his style of some of its youthful crudities. But he never showed any sign of acquiescence in Welhaven's critical standards, and, as will be seen, the strife was still raging in 1838, the year in which Sir Edmund detects a marked improvement. The fact is ignored that the poems published in 1833, "Caesaris," "Spaniolen," and most of the verses of "Digte, Anden Ring," have precisely the same characteristics as those which Welhaven made the object of his attack. Wergeland himself gives the year 1834 as the date when he first was able to distinguish good from bad, but there is no indication anywhere that this development was in any way due to the criticisms of his rival. That he could appreciate his opponent's verse is proved by his prefacing an article on the Norwegian landscape-painter J. C. Dahl with some lines from Welhaven's song to Dahl, 1839.

The year following the inception of the attack con-

tained two events in Wergeland's career which were not
without importance. It was in 1831 that on his way to
France he paid a short visit to England, where he formed
the impressions utilised at a much later date in his
remarkable poem—"The English Pilot." This was also
the year in which he became involved in the litigation
with Procurator Praëm which, spun out to incredible
lengths, lasted almost for the remainder of the poet's
life, and led to the financial embarrassment to which he
alludes in "Auktion over Grotten." (p. 187). The amusing
details of this case, which began by Wergeland's inser-
tion in Morgenbladet of an advertisement stigmatising
Praëm as a "criminal against the state and humanity,"
have been dealt with fully in Mr. Rolv Laache's recent
work,—"Henrik Wergeland og hans Strid med Pro-
kurator Praëm,"[1] and need not be further dwelt on
here, though the whole story, however tragic from the
point of view of the poet, is both characteristic and
entertaining.

A similar quixotism and lack of wordly wisdom marked
Wergeland's conduct a couple of years later, when he
was strenuously endeavouring to prevail upon the Church
Department to appoint him to a benefice. Though objec-
tion might possibly have been taken to his lack of theolo-
gical orthodoxy, this was not in fact, in that rationalistic
age, felt to be the obstacle. But Wergeland's applica-
tions were hopelessly prejudiced by the fact that he was
simultaneously engaged in political activities which could
not fail to be distasteful to the authorities. The poems
which were published in this year were steeped in revo-

[1] Vol I. Det Norske Videnskaps-Akademi, Oslo, 1927.

lutionary sentiment as a result of the July Revolution of 1830, and other events in the political arena of Europe. Not content with this, Wergeland at the same time undertook the editorship of a radical newspaper of bad repute—"Statsborgeren," and, when no active politician could be found to undertake the task, he attracted public attention by delivering the inaugurating speech at the unveiling of a monument to Christian Krogh, a patriot of a kind likely to be most distasteful to the authorities. It was therefore not surprising that his applications were uniformly unsuccessful, so much so that in the following year he had so far lost hope of ecclesiastical preferment as to begin the serious study of medicine with a view to adopting the profession of a doctor. It is to this side of his activities that we owe the poem "Pigen paa Ana-tomi-Kammeret" (p. 47). But this alteration of plans led to no practical result, for in 1836 he sought and obtained a post as assistant in the University Library, which supplied him for the moment with some sort of a living.

Meantime the controversy inaugurated by Welhaven had not ceased to convulse the minds of literary Norway, which was sharply divided into two opposing camps. Welhaven, however, had lost popularity in 1834 after the publication of his poem "Norges Dæmring" (the Dawn of Norway), wherein he vigorously satirised the narrow nationalism of that section of the population which formed his rival's principal support. In 1838, the tide for a moment definitely turned, when the Welhaven party made an unsuccessful attempt at organised disturbance on the occasion of the performance of Wergeland's piece "Campbellerne,"—a poor enough work on its own merits, though redeemed by the fine prologue, "Den første Gang," translated on p. 53. The merits of the play were however of secondary importance: "Campbellerne" was merely the bone of contention over which the two opposing factions tried their strength,—to the ignominious defeat of the anti-Wergeland forces. This was the high-water-mark of Wergeland's popularity and prosperity. For the moment, he was on the full tide of fortune. With the money which he had earned from the performance of "Campbellerne," he bought a small house, and the arrangements in connection with this venture brought hin into touch with his future wife, Amalie Bekkevold, the daughter of a local boatman. In August they became engaged, and before the end of the year the publication of the fine welcome to King Carl Johan, "Kongens Ankomst," (The King's Arrival), procured for the author such interest in the highest quarters that he was informally told that an application which he had sent for the vacant curacy of Nannestad was destined to be successful.

But the tide was soon to turn. With characteristic imprudence the poet with a couple of German acquaintances dropped in one evening on the Palace guard, and indulged in festivities the impropriety of which did not fail to be represented in exaggerated terms to the King. All hope of the expected benefice faded at once into the "beautiful clouds" in which Wergeland has enshrined his disappointment (p. 73). So far as Bernadotte was concerned, the effects of his resentment were short-lived, for a month after the episode he offered the poet a pension from his privy purse. This was accepted, on condition that it should be employed in work for the enlightenment of the populace, a task which had for a long time, and in many forms, absorbed no little share of Wergeland's monumental industry.

The results of acceptance were, however, of a most disastrous character. It is possible for us, at the present day, to explain the apparent inconsistency of the democratic revolutionary as a royal pensioner. Carl Johan was to Wergeland, as Napoleon had been before him, a figure of the French Revolution. He saw the promoted ranker rather than the somewhat autocratic and intriguing monarch. We may remember, too, how Nicolai Wergeland had all along advocated the union with Sweden, seeing the liberty of his country rather in the emancipation from the Danish yoke than in any complete independence. It was, moreover, a quite justifiable attitude for a democrat to see his real opponents rather in the national bureaucracy than in the crown. There can be no doubt that Wergeland was as sincere in his advocacy of popular liberty as he undoubtedly was in his admiration and affection for the person of the King. But his attitude was inevitably misunderstood. To his former supporters and friends he appeared as a venal traitor, while in fashionable and court circles, apart from the King himself, his popularity had long ago been irretrievably prejudiced. Wergeland found himself banned in all quarters. His pathetic poem „Fordums Venner" (p. 105), addressed to his former friend Ludvig Daa, expresses the depth of his depression at the unforeseen result of his action. His only consolation was in the affection of his wife, who had been the inspiration of the "Poesier" published in the previous year, and whom he married a month after the receipt of the fatal pension.

Yet from a financial point of view his position improved shortly afterwards, when he was appointed Keeper of the Norwegian Records, which were then housed in gloomy, dank and draughty rooms in the old fortress of Akershus. He entered upon his new duties in the New Year of 1841, and in the same year bought a new house, the celebrated "Grotten," on the borders of the royal park, and made use of the exceptional opportunities which his post afforded in composing his "Constitutional History of Norway." Of other important works written during this period, "Jan van Huysums Blomsterstykke," considered by some competent critics his finest work, was published in 1840, and was followed by "Svalen" in 1841. In the following year appeared the dialect poems entitled "Langeleiken" (from a national musical instrument in use among the peasantry), and his first propagandist efforts on behalf of the excluded Jews, the fine group of poems grouped under the common title of „Jøden" (the Jew).

Wergeland's promotion to his official post was, however, destined to prove fatal to him. To a less careless man it would, indeed, have been without danger, but in the spring of 1844, exposure without precaution to the severe climatic conditions of the Akershus cellars affected his lungs, and the damage was aggravated by his characteristic insistence on attending the national celebrations on the 17th of May, with impaired health and in inclement weather. At the same time, the ruin consequent on his protracted litigation with Praëm was consummated, and though the poem, "Auktion over Grotten," which he sent at this time to a loyal friend, does not represent an actual incident in his career, it was an anticipation which nothing but the generosity of the friend in question prevented from being actually realized, and he had in fact, before his death, to be removed to less expensive quarters. Finally, the year was further saddened by the illness and death of his friend and hero, the King, Carl Johan.

The courage and energy with which the dying poet met this series of catastrophes have perhaps induced too sentimental an estimate of the work of his last phase. In spite of the phenomenal industry which characterized the whole of his life, the output from the sickbed, where he lay for the greater part of a year in hopeless case, altogether surpassed all previous efforts. To this period belong "The English Pilot," a poem of special interest to this country, which has made a plot of the most crudely melodramatic kind the vehicle for lyrical passages of the utmost beauty, with descriptions of the country which he had visited, for a few days, once only, many years before, which are deservedly immortal. "Jødinden" (the Jewess), Wergeland's final effort for the Jewish cause, belongs to the same period, and, as he declared in the verses "Paa Sygeleiet" (p. 146), was intended to be indefinitely expanded, if death could be sufficiently long delayed. But besides these and other poems, such as the famous adress of the dying poet to his wallflower, and his appeal to his beloved springtime to save him (p. 196), Wergeland, in the last few months of his life, carried out the complete revision of his early epic, "Skabelsen, Mennesket og Messias," which was published under the title of "Mennesket." To this work he attached special importance, since he regarded it as containing his principal contribution to the problem of life, and hoped that, purged of its youthful crudities it might appeal to a wider public. [The perfection attained by man at the end of the first, youthful version is now put off for a few centuries, when Earth has become like Paradise, and Man glorious. Abiriel's glowing fire is blended in the race with the mild spirit of Ohebiel. In the charm of woman, however, wholly dwells Ohebiel's spirit, heavenly pure, whilst the flames of Abiriel flash stronger from the man, even as the diamond's core of light. The mighty spirit of Man now no longer feels its flesh and blood as a chain on its hands and a bolt at its foot. Like the feathers of birds merely, and a rose-leaf garb, does it feel the weight of its body. The bright day of Truth, the voices of Duty, and the wing-beat of Freedom triumphant over treacherous desire, fill the temple of his brow, while in his heart glows the fire of Brother-love, radiant from his outstretched hands.] I. G.

He also composed and completed the humorous auto-biographical notes to which he gave the name "Hassel-nødder" (hazel-nuts). For Wergeland to compose an auto-biography was, however, an almost superfluous task. Few poets have put more of themselves and the changes and chances of their lives into their work than he. There is hardly an important event in his life to which an allusion cannot be traced in his poetry. The last poems are particularly self-revealing. The bitterness with which he felt the defection of friends and adherents pierces through the courageous words in which he tries to show a brave face to the world. But there is enough of genuine courage and confidence as well, and he is always true to himself and never conventional. He was not the only poet to compose a fine farewell on his death-bed. The verses which Ewald, the Danish poet, wrote a few hours before his decease are deservedly famous. But they present a remarkable contrast to Wergeland's wall-flower poem, or his appeal to spring. Here is Ewald's poem:—

> Hero of Golgotha, to arms!
> Lift high thy blood-red shield;
> For sin's dark powers, with death's alarms,
> Against me take the field.
>
> Stretch out in wrath thy battle-brand
> Gainst those that strive with thee,
> And hurl them with thy mighty hand
> Down from the light, and me.
>
> Then shall I, safe in thy control,
> Meet death without dismay,
> Offering to thee my ransomed soul
> Upon its broken clay.
>
> Lord, grant me ease from pain and care,
> But, if thy chastenings smart,
> Teach me to trust, to pray, to bear,
> And Jesus fill my heart.

Wergeland's corresponding verses will be found on p. 198. We may note first how, while the imagery of Ewald's verses is drawn from ancient chivalry, Wergeland characteristically expresses himself in terms of nature-worship. The Danish poet utters a poignant and terror-stricken cry for help: Wergeland, in spite of an obvious desire for life and further usefulness, displays the serene confidence of one who feels, with Shelley, that

"the pure spirit shall flow
Back to the burning fountain whence it came,
A portion of the Eternal, which must glow
Through time and change, unquenchably the same."

He merely asks a friend to do him some slight service, and to convey his farewell messages, and the friend is, characteristically, neither human nor divine, but one of the children of his beloved Nature—a flower.

On the 12th of July, 1845, Wergeland's brief but busy life was ended, and his funeral on the 17th was attended by a huge concourse of admirers, who had at last learned something of the genius whom they had so long rejected. But especially the common people in a body followed the hearse of their friend. Since that day the reputation of the poet in his own country has continuously grown, and may now be said to be immoveably established. It is a more difficult task for us to estimate his place in the world-literature of his age.

In order to appreciate him, we must understand and sympathise with his conception of the poet's call,—a dedication of his special talent to the service of his nation and of mankind. For the kind of thing which, in criticising Danish poetry he called "sofa literature"—something to be enjoyed for its own beauty without rousing the reader to action—he had no use. "The ancient bards," he said, "kindled their listeners to perform great deeds, they did

not lock their souls up in cabinets, but went to their
work in the world. They lived in spheres which their
times did not yet touch, and their songs were prophe-
cies. . . . We do not want poets who live in Heaven, to
spit on the earth from it, but men who are masters of
their ideals, and who idealize in order to realize. . . .
The true poet can only belong to one party, that of
Heaven and a bettered earth."[1] Just as he conceived of
heavenly spirits raising humanity towards God by
sacrificially imprisoning themselves in the mortal bodies
of men and women, so he felt it to be the poet's duty
to forsake the transcendental beauties vouchsafed to his
privileged vision, except in so far as by working among
his fellow men he could bring them to aspire towards
them. His aim was not so much decorative as prophetic.
To the pure artist it matters supremely if, by the inclu-
sion of some irrelevant detail he disturbs the balance of
his work; to the orator or the prophet it is of little conse-
quence if some passage of his utterance falls below the
highest level, provided he can awaken eyes to see and
ears to hear. And in a country as poverty-stricken and
unenlightened as he felt the contemporary Norway to
be, there was so much to be said and done, and so little
time for the gigantic task before him. We need not
wonder, then, at the superficial faults which provide the

---

[1] Cf. Shelley, in his "Defence of Poetry": "For he (the poet)
not only beholds intensely the present as it is, and dis-
covers those laws according to which present things
ought to be ordered, but he beholds the future in the pre-
sent, and his thoughts are the germs of the flower and
the fruit of latest time." I. G.

critic with a facile excuse for a depreciatory verdict,—the chaotic flood of imagery and the desperate and frequently disastrous efforts of the poet to cram a dozen different pictures into the frame of a single sentence. Of such defects Wergeland himself was perfectly conscious. With a smile he confesses that

"By parentheses unnumbered
The reader is encumbered;
But also for the author they are horns
Entangling him like Abram's ram in thorns,
Ever more hopelessly, in sorry trim,
Where he won't get his thought, but the critic will get him."[1]

A further reason for this lack of clarity is that his vision is too all-embracing. As Mr. Grøndahl has happily expressed it, "by means of the 'yellow spot' in the background of the eye, we see one thing in one moment while the surrounding objects merge into vagueness. In Wergeland the whole background of the eye is golden, and when all that has been gathered there is to be rendered in the long succession of written words, the lines may often take on the shape of a maze—always, however, with something at the centre worth the search."[2] Wergeland is too much himself to be an easy subject for comparisons. It is true that critics such as Vullum have shown some ingenuity in endeavouring to establish the paradox that the art of Wergeland was built, without violent transition, upon that of his predecessors. It is never difficult, by a process of selection, to suggest a

[1] Translated by Mr. Grøndahl, *Chapters in Norwegian Literature*, p. 57.
[2] Ibid: pp. 57, 58.

resemblance, but we are reminded of the visitor to India who identified an elephant with her friend's description of a mosquito! No one who opened "Digte, første Ring" could have felt for an instant that he was reading the work of a Zetlitz, a Schwach or a Bjerregaard. The outstanding feature was a complete and unmistakeable break with all national tradition.

Owing perhaps to his rejection of the mediaevalism which so strongly influenced Teutonic literature, he seems more akin to some of our British poets than to those of his own country or lands adjacent to it. The temporary influence of Byron has been touched on already: in his youth, indeed, Wergeland was often spoken of as a Norwegian Byron, but the resemblance, as Latham remarks, was never very close, and in later years was imperceptible. As a democrat and a poet of the people, he clearly felt a kinship with Burns, many of whose songs he translated; but, except in so far as he followed the Scottish poet in basing many of his verses on popular folk-tunes, his sympathy with the man did not result in any marked community of style or thought. Probably his imperfect grasp of the language hindered any closer affinity; there are at least three definite mistranslations in his version of "Mary Morison," and we can see from "the English Pilot" that he never really mastered English—to say nothing of Scotch!

The resemblances which strike one most are often to poets whose work, in all probability, he had never read. Not infrequently we are vividly reminded of Blake, but Wergeland, in spite of Welhaven's assertion, was eminently sane and even practical in his writings; in spite of some suggestions of mystic experience, as in "Svalen," there was little of the mystic temperament about him, and for all his love of imagery he eschewed symbolism. In Wordsworth we find the essence of Wergeland's nature-gospel expressed in such passages as that in "Tintern Abbey"—

> "a sense sublime
> Of something far more deeply interfused,
> Whose dwelling is the light of setting suns,
> And the round ocean and the living air,
> And the blue sky, and in the mind of man:
> A motion and a spirit, that impels
> All thinking things, all objects of all thought,
> And rolls through all things" . . .

But while this deeper nature-philosophy is evidently shared by Wergeland, his habitual reaction to the beauties of the world about him is something far more direct and simple. He retains to the last that unquestioning joy in the mere outward appearance of such things which in Wordsworth faded with the passing years. The delight which impelled him to song in

> "The scarlet on an insect's wing"

had in it all the unreasoning pleasure of a child. He never had mournfully to acknowledge that

> "nothing can bring back the hour
> Of splendour in the grass, of glory in the flower."

His perception of just such things remained an abiding inspiration, not something which evoked

> "Thoughts that do often lie too deep for tears."

The butterfly which he adressed called forth his love and sympathy for its own sake; he could never have said, like Wordsworth,

> "Thou bring'st, gay Creature as thou art!
> A solemn image to my heart,
> My Father's Family!"

It is even extremely doubtful whether Wordsworth's poetry would have appealed to Wergeland: certainly he would have repudiated the English poet's dictum—which is exactly in the spirit of Welhaven—that "poetry takes its origin from emotion recollected in tranquillity;" his fiery and uncontrollable Muse responded rather to the stimulus of a present emotion at boiling point. Tranquillity is the last quality which anyone would dream of attributing to Wergeland. Even where he expresses himself as having found peace, as in "I det Grønne" and "Paa Sygeleiet," the reader cannot fail to notice how full his mind is of the disturbing emotions which he affects to have overcome. Like his spiritual successor, Bjørnson, he was a born fighter, full of the joy of battle; as he somewhere remarks, "A fighting existence is delightful when one has a beak!"

He has been more often compared with Shelley, of whom, indeed, he may have heard, as his English friend, Latham, frequently mentions him. In Shelley, as in Wordsworth, we find the Wergelandian idea of the spiritual unity in Nature:—

> "that sustaining Love
> Which, through the web of being blindly wove
> By man and beast and earth and air and sea,
> Burns bright or dim, as each are mirrors of
> The fire for which all thirst" . . .

The political views of Shelley are also remarkably akin
to those of the Norwegian poet: both men shared a
burning hatred of tyranny, and sympathised with all
their souls in the contemporary aspiration towards
liberty of every kind. But here again, there is no reason
for suspecting any direct influence: such thoughts were
in the air. The differences between the work of Shelley
and Wergeland are no less striking than the resemblances.
In spite of the troubles which beset his life, there was a
robust light-heartedness, a humorous pluck, and an un-
conquerable hopefulness about Wergeland. He could
never have thought or written—

> "Most wretched men
> Are cradled into poetry by wrong:
> They learn in suffering what they teach in song."

Wergeland declares that the heart is strengthened by
suffering, as the arm is by fighting, and as the voice is
raised in the storm. But really, one feels on reflection,
between the cultured and ethereal flow of Shelley and
the peaks and abysses of Wergeland's unregulated in-
spiration there can be few points of contact to invite
comparison. It would be hardly more futile to compare
the painting of Botticelli with that of Rembrandt.

The direct influence of others upon Wergeland's work
is, in fact, almost negligible. My friend Mr. Grøndahl,
in his lectures, has indicated resemblances as close as
any hitherto referred to in the work of later and ob-
viously independent writers—Mazzini, patriot and cos-
mopolitan, Whitman, Edward Carpenter, and Tagore.
He has also traced most interesting analogies in the
career and writings of Giordano Bruno, although any

connection between the 19th century Norwegian and the
16th century Italian must necessarily have been of the
most remote and indirect kind, filtered perhaps through
Spinoza, whom Wergeland at one time studied.[1] After
all, we must conclude, Wergeland was first and foremost
an original character: the merits and defects of his art
both arise from its spontaneity. There was no per-
ceptible line between the poet and the man. As he
panegyrised Nature in all her aspects in his verse, so
he kept a menagerie of pets, ranging from his pony,
Veslebrunen (Brownie), to a one-eared and three-legged
rabbit, and carried about beech-mast in his pocket to
sow in any suitable spot which he might come across
in his wanderings. The feverish industry with which he
wrote during the last months of his life did not prevent
him from remembering to distribute seeds and vegetables
to the cottars around Eidsvoll. So too, his poetry is a
natural expression of his mind. It is characteristic of
him that he so often interposes prose passages in his
poems, or begins, as in "Kaadt Ukrudt," in a conversa-
tional style that may be verse, but can hardly be called
poetry. He is just talking—and then he gets excited,
and sings. As the emotion rises, inspiration descends on
him in a flood, till he can hardly get out what he wants
to say. His is then the ecstasy described in the passage
which we have selected from "Jan van Huysums Blomster-
stykke" (p. 74),—and the language becomes

[1] The watchword of this type of man has perhaps been best
given by Victor Hugo: Nous qui parlons ici, nous ne croyons
à rien hors de Dieu. Cela dit, continuons." ("William
Shakespeare", Ed. Nelson, p. 40). I. G.

> "Brudte, vilde ord (og dog
> Skjønne som af Salighedens
> Ubekjendte himmelsprog)."

It may not always be first-rate poetry, but it is perfect self-expression. It is like the torrent in spate, necessarily turbid, and carrying along with it a lot of miscellaneous rubbish, but after all the mountain burn has beauties which we miss in the pellucid waters of a sluice-controlled chalk-stream. Of course, too, there were other and milder moods which found their natural expression in his poetry and on such occasions he is perhaps at his best. But he is always himself, meaning intensely every word he says. Much poetry that we read gives us the impression of a work of art as detached from its creator as a painting or a sculpture; Wergeland always conveys the illusion of the spoken voice,—he seems to be talking to us. That is perhaps the great secret of his continued influence;— "He being dead yet speaketh."

*

The aim of this book is to give to English readers unacquainted with the Norwegian language a general view of the poetry of Henrik Wergeland. The selection is not intended to be an anthology of his best work only, but rather to illustrate the characteristic features of his thought, his temper and his style, at all stages of his career. Translation is a compromise, in the effecting of which something is bound to be lost, and it is felt that characteristics can be more adequately rendered than beauties, some of which must necessarily be restricted to the language of the original. It is believed, however, that most of the poetical work on which Wergeland's reputation rests will be found to be included, at least in extracts.

Substantially, the metres of the original poems have been retained in the translations. Dissyllabic endings, in which the Norwegian language is more rich than ours, have in many cases been represented by monosyllabic. In poems such as "Den Engelske Lods" (The English Pilot), in which the rhymes are often widely separated and the rhyming system quite unsystematic, it has seemed quite futile to try to retain this arbitrary order exactly. It happens, however, in „Til Min Hustru" (To My Wife), that the order of the rhymes is almost if not quite identical. In "Et Gammelnorskt Herre-sæde" (A Viking's Hall), the translation is not quite in the metre of the original, but seeks to preserve its general character.

In the experiment in dialect from "Langeleiken," place-names as well as language have been altered from Norwegian to Scottish; otherwise the versions are believed to be faithful renderings, with which no unnecessary liberties have been taken.

The translations for which Mr. Grøndahl is responsible have been extensively revised, but do not appear in print for the first time, having been issued in a privately printed volume in 1919, through the kindly interest of Mr. F. W. Chapman of Gosforth, Newcastle-on-Tyne, who has also effectively helped in the present under-taking. Some of them will also be found in "Chapters in Norwegian Literature," published by Gyldendal in 1923. My own translations are for the most part new, though a large part of "Følg Kaldet" (Follow the Call), the first verse of Welhaven's satire, given in the introduction, and perhaps a stray verse besides, appeared in my volume "Norway" (the Modern World series, Benn, 1925) and are reprinted with the permission of the publishers. None of Mr. Bithell's contributions have hitherto been published.

The originating idea of the book is Mr. Grøndahl's: we contribute to a scheme in which he has been throughout the moving spirit. Speaking for myself, I wish to acknowledge the kind and continuous help received from Mr. Grøndahl; my translations, as they were drafted, were invariably submitted, singly or in batches, to his helpful criticism, to which any merit which they may possess must in no small measure be attributed. As, however, I was frequently recalcitrant and persisted in adhering to my own opinions, I must be held fully responsible for any shortcomings.

According to our original plan, the introduction was to have been written by Mr. Grøndahl, and only the circumstance that he was prevented by pressure of work and other reasons from proceeding with the task has caused it to devolve upon me, with such assistance as he has been able to afford me. While it is to be regretted that Mr. Grøndahl's enthusiastic sympathy with the subject has not been more directly available, it is perhaps appropriate, in a work of this kind, that an Englishman rather than a Norwegian should pay his tribute to the genius of Wergeland, which in Norway is too generally acknowledged to be in need of further recognition from his compatriots, while outside Scandinavia and Scandinavian North America he is hardly known at all. "I was—and that was my misfortune with a language so isolated—nothing but a poet."

G. M. Gathorne-Hardy.

HENRIK WERGELAND TO THE DECEASED PETER KREFTING, HIS FRIEND [1]

(Transl. by I. Grøndahl.)

Ah! how the stars are sparkling: my friend's
Spirit is now passing by,
Onward to swell the
Crowd of the spirits.

Now it glided 'twixt me and a star,
As from the altar the blue
Incense before the
High-lifted torches.

Death's couch (alas!) the altar, and lo!
Phthisis the priestess, whose knife
Ever is blunt, yet
Sure and thirsty.

Ha! I will mock at Fate, who shall now
Nought find in me any more,
Nought that her questing
Finger may probe for.

Fools can only curse Fate; as for me,
Coward I call him: he flees,
When neath the lyrical
Ivy I rustle—

[1] Henrik Wergeland til den døde Peter Krefting, hans
Ven, 1827.

Leaves his fingers grasping shall miss;
They are the garb of my soul,
Inwoven in thy
Memory, Dead One!

Fearless and faithful futureward look—
Such is the glittering wand,
That which determines
Fate's every footstep.

Reek not dim vapour from my heart-string
Sooner a ray I will send,
After the spirit
Send a ray sooner.

Now canst thou learn the lay of the worlds,
Now—like a butterfly on
Heaven's full roses,
Star-clusters, clinging—

Draw pure the honey given to man
Fouled in the ancient horn,
Writhing with darksome
Hieroglyphics.

See'st thou thy friend? Cheek resting on hand,
Neither in sorrow nor joy
To an Æolian
Harp does he listen.

Was it thy spirit floating upon
Waves of the breath-fondled gold?
Was it a wind which
Kissed my brow lightly?

Spheres are thy harp: to silvery strings,
Stretched on the infinite blue
Shield-rims of Heaven,
Now canst thou listen!

When to thy friend came the news of thy death,
Stars shot from Heaven; they came
Hasting to hail the
New-comer welcome,

As from the lake a white-breasted flock,
Swans towards the first breath of spring,
Clamorous rise on
Pinions extended.

Venus then sent, forth-beaming, a sweet
White-veiled Stella, a guide
To the good beings'
Star to escort thee.

Mars hurled a beam, a herald gold-helm'd,
Bidding thy soul come and join
High on his car the
Host of his heroes.

Charles' Wain—a dancing chorus of fair
Vestals advancing, and great
Genial Rhea
Sylvia leading—

Choose rather thou! See, far toward the Pole
Rolls around midnight its wheel;
With lily finger
Points the high priestess.

Linger till I, a fluttering veil,
Or a faint luminous cloud,
Come to thee drifting
Over the mountains!

Lo, we shall melt together to one
Conscious being—two rays
Gold-winged Aurora
Boreal forming!

High-hearted wert thou, free was thy soul:
White-toothed wave did it hurl
Hard 'gainst the rock of
Tyranny, hollowed.

Warm for thy land, the rights of all men,
Thou every tyrant didst hate,
Whether a sceptre
Or a pen wielding.

Friend! a birth merely to thee was thy death:
Little the child knows the pangs
Felt by its mother—
Life was thy mother.

Reek not dim vapour from my heart-string!
Sooner a ray I will send
After the spirit,
Out of tears beaming.

Song is its wing, and so it will not
Drown in the cloud-deeps without
Reaching at last thy
Hastening shadow!

From MY LITTLE RABBIT [1]
(Transl. by G. M. Gathorne-Hardy.)

BUNNY, when your studious friend
Lonely o'er that book did bend,
Sacred to the Jews of old,
Claiming too the title bold—
"Source of life and Heaven's ascent",
(Overscored with hieroglyphs,
Penned with blood and logogryphs)—
—Hurled it then so far away
That he found it not to-day,
Fancying that his harp's spread wing
Swifter far his soul would bring
Heavenward through the firmament
Than those yellow parchment bags
Overfilled with musty tags;—
And his humble lyre did take
The oppressive hush to break,
While you, little bunny mine,
Sported where the moonbeams shine,
(As a child with coins might play)
On my floor, and chuckled gay
When you heard my sounding string
Over all the gamut ring:
How you pricked your ear, to show
Your dislike for notes of woe!
Waved that silky topknot, just
As you meant away to thrust
Every sound of grief that came—

[1] Min lille Kanin. From Digte 1ste Ring, 1829.

Like a funeral's dark parade
From a palace colonnade—
From the harp's resplendent frame.
When with skip and jump around
You in loops and rings did bound,
And across the moonlight flew,
Like a cloud when heaven is blue,
Drifting on the merry breezes
Wheresoe'er its spirit pleases,
Through the zenith, past the sun,
Dark and free and full of fun:
Then life's source I seemed to see
In my corner, like a brook
Sprinkling all its drops on me,
Clearer far than in my book.
In my little bunny grey
I could see a drop of spray;
And I took it up, and pressed
Like a teardrop to my breast,
Like a tear, which Nature's eye
Shed on me from sympathy,
When she saw how grief could plough
Early furrows on my brow.
Then that tear so close I pressed,
Bunny, to my grateful breast
—That which Nature on me shed—
That it broke in two, and spread
Like a vapour soft and blue,
Covering all things as it grew;
Earth below and Heaven on high,
Creeping beast and starry sky;

Blending with the Milky Way
Deeps and all that in them lay.
All things melted and were part
Of that tear-cloud's mighty heart,
Sea and land and mountain tops
Faded into hueless drops.
Yet their shape they all retained;
Sun was sun of steam—a black
Vapour in the midnight wrack—
But the snake a snake remained,
Like a streak with writhe and twist.
(Lo! 'twas thus I seemed to see
The Creator's fantasy.)
I into that sea of mist
Dropped in likeness of a tear,
Where, of light and hue bereft,
Sun and worm in nebulous weft
Blending seemed to disappear.
Then was granted to my seeing
Insight into life and being!
Like a lightning gleam in cloud,
Burst a misty orb in flame;
Soon a thousand others glowed,
Colour, air, and water came!
Mete and bound and zone and pole
O'er those myriad suns did roll.
Of their fire the smoke was air,
From its light sprang colour's play,
Through those vapours vague and rare
Blood and earth impelled their way:
Round about the suns they flew;

Thence the worlds and heavens grew.
So the eternal process runs,
Suns shall light unkindlèd suns,
Still in shrouded heavens astray,
Sleeping o'er the Milky Way.

NAPOLEON [1]
(Transl. by J. Bithell.)

SPIRITS sublime are the swans in the galaxy,
Nile of Heaven, where the glittering
Stars are drops, and planets
   Pearls in the trough of it,
Shooting stars spume upleaping,
When by the pinions of spirits
   Struck is the wave.

We are the germs in the slime left by spirits;
Souls unfold like the butterfly
Out of the chrysalis, heightening
   Power of spirits:
Higher and higher, through spirals,
Rises the army of spirits
   Up to God.

Fain to increase are spirits, beholding
Here the virtuous, mighty
Soul unwind from the dust-slough:
   Ready then, like an eagle,
Shaking rime from his plumage,
Sin to cast and interpret
   Life's rhythmic anthem.

[1] Napoleon. From Digte 1ste Ring, 1829.

Spirits (like beams shooting down into
Clammy mould, then ascending
Like a long glittering yellow-green
    Palm) into boyhood's
Body descend, and shoot up then
Into deeds which are flowers and
    Fruit of the soul.

Woman, in the sleepy lamplight parturient,
Hears with a quivering joy her first-born's
Cry: she can scarce foreshadow
    He is a spirit
Fallen in the embryo's earth-soul,
Even as in Danae's lap that
    Gold-gleaming rain.

Often a spirit dives into different
Hearts, and the wondering
World sees its face with sudden
    Laurels spread, while the olive
Blooms in the oak-tree's shadow,
Mid the long lyric ivy's
    Pallid green.

(Hear Albuquerque's sword! Where the Indians
Flee, like clouds 'fore the curvèd
Moon! See Henry the Sailor
    Pensively tracing
Ribs of a country in Gambian
Sand! Hear Camoens' darkling
    Harp tempestuous!)

Centuries fade into mist ere a genius
Into a soul descends whole: then
Nations shake with the visible
   Grasp of God in the universe;
Minds then of multitudes billow,
Like, when the north wind sweeps o'er them,
   Corn-ears curving.

Such was the soul that in actions
Shot forth from Roman Julius,
As from Lebanon's fertile
   Valleys, in cedars,
Beams with the sun warm, like obelisks:
Then lay the vast world beneath the
   Shadow of Caesar.

Unto Britain a genius was
Heaven-sent in Shakespeare. Times ancient
Mirrored his soul, as a spring does
   Oaks mossed and hoary.
Schemes of Kings in the poet's
Fata Morgana the earth saw,
   Awed into terror.

Gods of the ancients were spirits
God sent to earth, in the earth's dress
Clad, to tread out the firstling
   Footsteps of reason.
Well might the first-born marvel,
Dizzy as though they awakened
   Out of a dream.

Resteth antiquity—sea-calm: memories
See we as sails or as stars are
On the horizon; the Middle
   Somnolent Ages,
Sleepy-waved with tides crawling,
Sigh as they cradle crimson
   Riven sails.

Now seethes the present, like ocean round
Stromboli: sweating the wave must
Leave its vain toil and stifle not
   Fire in the sea-deeps:
Snorting the flames are: their heavy
Breath you see on the billows'
   Back as fleeces.

Forth from time shot Napoleon, as from
Ocean a palm-clad Delos.
Freedom was the Latona,
   Which behind his
Victory's palms bore him gladly
Fortune and fame as Latona bore
   Dian and Phoebus.

Hail to thee, genius! sent hither
Europe's crashed snake-ship to pilot!
Nations hearkened, as children
   Hearken the tempest,
When it with crowns of fir-trees
Plays, in the dust smiting
   Cupola towers.

Kings sat on thrones, like vultures
Clinging to nests, with their plumage
Craven and bursten, with stiffened
   Gaze, and with open
Beaks, when they hear the golden
Eagle's wings beat the swollen
   Cloud afar.

Pale the Saracen saw not the Pyramids,
Knew no more his run to the desert—
Feet no more found the track of it,
   For it was hid by
Pale red blood-steam of hecatombs;
Hotter from Himalaya
   Ganges sprang.

Nelson, like fabled Fafnir on gold crouched,
Lay with his eyes fixed on Orient's
Swelling ocean of purple,
   Lay like the negro
Curbing his lance and waiting
Till o'er the plain from the palm-grove
   Paces the lion.

Swifter he flies, bent-backed, than a
Feathered arrow: his roaring
Rolls from the hills round the hunter's
   Ears: from the Alps rang
Thus the echo of victory
Almost unto the anger-filled
   Sails of the Britons

Ha! how the tribe of Tarquin when
Brutus woke trembled! how they shook behind
Hedges of slaves before him, whose
   Host was a flock of
Singing friends who tore the
Hedges down, when behind them
   Laurels shone!

See how the storm-wind of minds he governed!
See how the Danube darkens!
Kings to their orb are clinging:
   Nations laugh, and
Yearningly wait to see it
Driving come to them like a
   Soap-bubble.

Greater than western Timoleon-Bolivar,
Concepts of freedom for nations
His thyrsus formed, hanging like
   Northern lights crackling
(Fair as shadows in Hellas)
High uplifted o'er blanching
   Foreheads of kings.

Bloody dreams of the nations'
Vengeance now monarchs saw real,
Storming of thrones and grasping of crowns like
   Grape-bunches pendent.
Crowns were the lure of the lightning
Whenas Napoleon's sword flashed,
   Lightning itself.

Cloud-wrapt in joy and the nations'
Longings, the swish of Napoleon's
Sword was the Be! of ideas: his
   Sword framed republics,
Even as Thorvaldsen's chisel
Hector's marble, the features
   Bold of Prometheus.

(Was not Parthenope's state like
Helena's billowing bosom?
Was not Rome's free state Paris the
   Hermaphrodite?
Hector's swelling white muscles
Did they not bear the Cisalpine
   State of the free?)

Like fiery locks in the comet's trail,
Heroes flocked in the Consul's
Footsteps, Ney that Sertorius,
   Scipio Eugene was,
And Pontecorvo's sword-glint
Flew over Germany like sparks from
   Hecla erupting.

Answer me, Cato-Carnot, whether Gaul's love
Offered to him the pallium?
Grasped his ambition? Was not
   Glory his flashing
Pallium?—Ah thou art pointing
Pale to the shadows of Caesar and
   Antony!

Spain's throes stayed not the Emperor,
Though she clung, vengeance-mad, like the
Crab at Hercules' heel when with
  Eyes flashing onward he
Smote the monster
Frothing in blood behind the
  Reeds of the Danube.

Prussia was like the youth that, fleeing,
Hurls his lance, and for life's sake
Leaves behind him his buckler:
  Pale-faced peeps he
Into his virulent mother's
Room, backward casting
  Frightened looks.

Earth with terror sees Pitt's and Britain's
Plans like bloody shadows
Hovering in mists that France's
  Eagle is cleaving:
Nations shudder like children staring at
Serpents rearing behind a
  Gilded grating.

Kings, like globes round the sun, gather round him:
At his command free ocean
Will no more bear the heavy
  British banner
Stiff with gore: he commands, and
Poland's sighs turn to spears in
  Russia's breast.

Plans like sunbeams his soul flashed, and they
Deep in the fogs of Siberia
Drowned: ah! every thought of his
   Flew with steel nibbed,
What time he against tyranny's
Timurbeg's-pyramid
   Bade forth the storm.

Europe's soul was he, and the nations
Seemed his brawn, when, like Samson
Under the idol's temple,
   He the pyramid
Raised on necks forged in slavery,
Grim as a fog-bound mountain,
   Bade burst asunder.

Darkening Europe, it challenged him:
Broadening the base was, under
Stones groaned Poland.
   Nations he saw now
Driven to the sea: he commanded, and
Steel-bright billows of heroes
   Onward rolled.

He like the tempest on billows sat,
When they, foam-specked, broke over Friedland,
When Smolensk, first of corner-stones,
   Shattered before them:
When Mojaisk's blood-mosaic
Showed in the split of it Moscow's
   Marble block.

Was it a fate that, under falling
Moscow, like the champion in Dagon's
Temple, Napoleon crushed?
   Ruled there a *fatum*
Over his spirit gigantic, and
Hurled him, like Phaeton,
    Down from the heavens?

O how bootless to hearken the
Spheres' starred harp with chill terror,
Dreaming that we are bound to
   Heaven's wheel of stars, as
Unto the wheels of a triumphing
Victor, believing us onward
    Whirled with the stars!

Man his fate fashions: the proud glance
On to the future is the
Shimmering staff that sketches
   Fate striding onwards:
Tempest begotten when mighty
Concepts cross one another
    Destiny is.

Casca's dagger, you think, was fate's finger
Pointed at Julius? Rather a bloody
Birth of the longing of Cassius for
   Freedom, and Caesar's
Longing to curb with the sceptre
Parthia's panther and Roma's
    Ravening wolf.

Love of his native land crossed in Cassius
Caesar's ambition like blue-black
Thunder-clouds: was it
    Fate, if Cassius'
Sulphur clouds lightning hurled? If the
Plans of Brutus gave wing to
    Casca's hand?

Strength to bear down the towering
Frame of Napoleon was given
But to the elements: tempests
Billows no longer can tumble
    When they are frozen.
Did he not know that ancient
Scythians fight with arrows
    White of the clouds?

Friends of his flee, leave his greatness
Bare as a tempest-blown forest
Down from the peak, like the mantle
    Blown from Herakles'
Corded nape: a greedy
Sea of swords in his footsteps
    Forward foams.

Now again they like reeds by the river shook,
When he, storm-wrapped in greatness,
Back to the shore of Seine's river
    Rolled like the thunder;
Even o'er Belle-Alliance's
Reddened fields his victory's
    Echo rang.

Lo! how he strode, like a demon
Out of the grave, from Elba!
Europe he shook, mid black shields of
  Ocean driving,
Mid the crowns of earth's kingdoms:
Fear of rulers did but
  Measure his greatness.

Nations that buried him living
(Kingdoms for him did a tomb build)
Sang: "To freedom we sacrifice!"
  —Had he then been
Earth's dictator? — With Brutus's
Face averted I cry to you:
  "Die! let him die!"

Ha! He is dead! His monument
Stands in the temple of memories:
Shrine in a temple!—The lofty
  Shield-covered pillars
Memories themselves are, and Saga
Basreliefs chisels upon the
  Vault of the arch.

Those spiral columns yonder
Earth's bards have raised and garlanded!
Great is his temple: for truth is
  Born on his sepulchre:
Over it memory to foster,
Fair, like the heart that broke, like the
  Spirit, mighty!

HYMN TO LIBERTY [1]
(Transl. by G. M. Gathorne-Hardy.)

THE Arab may sing of the deep that is gleaming with
   And Mahara's gold-dust;   [jewels,
Ne'er can he picture the Northern heavens,
Wreathed by the northern lights with a necklace
Of flame, like waves of his fancied
   Desert treasures.

So the poet, whose harp the Almighty has hung on
   In Herthadal,[2] only   [the beech-tree
Sings of a crown whose bygone glory
Faintly is mirrored from Norway's mountains:
That now worn by the yeomen of Norway
   Scarce he dreams of.

Ah, he looks askance, if a lyre should
   Glint through the pine-trees.
"Flows there yet silver in Norway's veins?
Or was it a waterfall? Keep thy water!"

Ah, is silver a country's blood? Then
   Norway is dead, since
Denmark's leech-swarms to Trondelag clung,
Hollow tentacles stabbing in Kongsberg's[3] breast.

Lo! now her isles lie scattered like lifeless leeches
   Upon their sluggish billows.

[1] Hymne til Friheden. Digte 1ste Ring, 1829.
[2] Herthadal = Denmark.
[3] Kongsberg. The Norwegian silver mines.

Liberty, Heaven's own breath, is downward wafted
   To heal my wounded country.
Lo! with light the poor man's cottage it filleth,
   Oh, as if Norway had grasped at
Heaven's basket of stars, to slake her thirst for
   Draughts which fail from her gutted mine-shafts.

Fain are we all to robe our pride in the raiment
Woven of melody; I too will name my
Fatherland's wealth, e'en the gold which flows in
   Veins of the Norsemen:
Jewels which spring from the Norseman's breast, and
Gleam in his eye, or his brow that the diadem
Shades, which brought to Publicola honour,
   That will I sing of.

O Liberty, God's breath which fills the angels,
O Liberty, a stream of the centuries
Awhirl with crowns and royal bones
Like spindrift round dismantled thrones,
And cowl of monk and crown of Pope
Like some black breaker's toppling slope,
   Smote thee either to Heaven, or
   Dragged thee down to Hell, for
   Since Brutus died,
And Caesar clutched at the Parthian's pride,
On earth thou wast not. In marble hall
Tyrant and hangman trampling on all,
Mid bolted gyves (as a spider lurks in the web he spun)
   Were free alone;
And the purple of Kings shed the only light
On a shuddering thraldom's dreadful night.

Then first we heard thou wast gliding found,
O Liberty, on Pennsylvania's streams,
In wild and palm-shadowed Indian forests:
    And Washington quaffed thee,
    And back so Britannia's
    Banners he blew,
    As if they had been
    Lord North's periwigs.

Whence camest thou? O Freedom, didst thou fly
Down from the oak the earth bore like a fan
O'er Franklin's cradle, till straightway
    His speech was the keen, cold
    Whistle of Washington's
    Sword, when it shore
    Summit and centre
    From crowns terrestrial?

Whence camest thou? O Freedom, didst thou rise
First (like a smiling mermaid from Mississippi)
From Washington's sword-bright stream of
    Eloquence, when thou
    Divedst from the Comitia,
    And to a new
    World, 'neath the Ocean
    Swam'st down the Tiber?

Ah, scarce I remembered how Liberty, pale
On her secret journey, the British shores did scale:
    For short rest was there,
    Where a dictator stood

On the soil yet bright with a tyrant's blood,
  While puritan prayer
  Darkened the air.
O, love for humanity is Freedom's heart,
Tolerance her smile to all men,
And if her glance of wrath is an edge of steel
Her look of peace is a glittering leaf of palm.

Ha! Next thou flewest to Gallia's cry: now
Despots flee from the people, the hate that
Licks their tracks with bloody and lolling
   Tongue, like a panther.

But Gallia, idolatrous overmuch,
Her new-found Freedom must handle and touch;
Her heart is cold, but her hand is pressed
To warm in the fugitive's haughty breast.
Hark! with their lips they call thee. Stay!
Freedom they hail as divine,
They raise her image in light of day,
While night in chains they twine.

Drunk in blood of Kings, Gallia unfastened
Liberty's belt, broke her crown in two like a wedding
Alas! before she was the nation's bride.   [ring,

Ah, when the belt of the chaste one was broken,
Issued no scent from her breast, but on bright wings
                       of laurel
The Emperor's black flock of eagles grim.

Who had forgot, when eagle Rome
  Grew golden crest
  And purple vest,
Both claw of steel and song she lost?

On towards the mountains, which covered with
                                centuries
The Norseman's champion sleeping, the heavenly one
Looked and wept then, but lo! her tears ꟼɘꟻ on
  Hearts reawakening,   [Norway's
(Hot fall a mother's tears on the hearts of her
Sons) and they struck: away flapped the vampire that
Drained them of blood . . . Far fled she, to batten on
  Slaves in their slumber.

The mountains of Norway are arched to a temple,
A home for Freedom the exile;
The waterfall's rainbow is the smoke of Liberty's
                              hearthstone.

(O come, dear mother, Hedemark is a lovely bed.)

Now like a breath of God Freedom is lodged behind
Dovre and Filefjeld's ranged pillars; Kringen
Stands in the midst, like the altar, bright with blood.

(O come, dear mother, let Toten be a fair field for thee.)

See Christiania's fjord, like a carpet of violets sprinkled
In festival up towards the portal,
Where, like a shield of peace, a crown is set up to adorn it.

(O come, dear mother, Trondelag is a wide cradle.)

Round the assembly-place angels with swords are
stationed,
Like eagles with wings wide extended,
Eager to capture Freedom, that breath of God.
(Like holy apostles, who sadly smile as they gather—
For woe was at Heaven's gates—the latest flame from
The wing-points of departing angels.)

O Freedom, hovering "Fiat" o'er the abyss
(As deep beneath thee as a throne is high)
Where nations are swarming . . .
    Hovering "Fiat," that criest—
        "Godhead, come
From the heart to earth thy home:
Come from palaces and hovels,
When thou first thy way hast trod
From folly blind, and grief that grovels,
From the rat-hole of selfishness,
Though soiled with earth, yet, yet progress
To Heaven's freedom here: to God.
Let not thyself be frightened down
By ermine robe or glittering crown,
Never must thou flee or quake
Either for sceptre or for stake,
Nor let a monkish robe of black
E'er have power to scare thee back!"

O Freedom, stay, that speakest so.
In the arched temple of this land
May Norsemen like their pine-trees grow,

Thy pillars, and our maidens be
Veiled images of Liberty,
Stamped with a glorious master's hand.

Freedom, by the dark wrath of Kings,
As radiant day by night, pursued,
Rest in my fatherland proud with Niobe's smile, and
Hang o'er the Norseman's humble doorway
Garlands of oak-leaves, and call to thy hearth thy
    Sons to inherit.

Breathe in the hearts of Hellas, and straight inflate
Up to mighty bucklers that hang upon   [them
Bloody hands, as the swollen storm-cloud on
    Castor and Pollux.

Let Eurotas, like Susquehannah,
Past exultant and peacefully gazing
Greeks (as a glittering sword before Liberty)
    Calmly be gliding.

And when I pray to thee, oppressed one,
I pray to God . . .
Thou art of Him, as of me my spirit that
Borrowed my heart for a cradle.

So in the worlds of Space (that are God's hearts
In His heavenly bosom)
Thou art fostered—O, like a blushing sea of
Baby spirits, that suck above us the milk-white
Starshine, food of immortality, hope,—
    There art thou resting.

FINAL HYMN FROM CAESARIS [1]

(Transl. by G. M. Gathorne-Hardy.)

Sure cycle of Justice, God's hand overruling art thou;
In the roar of thy thunder, O Father, thy spirit we
know:
The flames through the reek are but Wisdom's calm
smile 'neath her cloak;
The sparks from the sacrifice—eyes, that ascend to the
skies, and behold
How days that are brighter, and kingdoms and cities
more fair than of old
Laugh out past the ashes and smoke.
O brothers who perish, sing glory to God while we die!

Sure cycle of Justice, God's hand overruling art thou;
Thou plantedst the life in the deep, thou but prunest
thy bough:
Anew shall it flourish, and blossom arise from the sod.
The pestilence dark is an angel recruiting the armies
of God.
When the tempest has scattered our homes like a dust-
cloud, about us it flings
The plumes of a seraphin's wings.
O brothers who perish, sing glory to God while we die!

God's hand—and shalt thou, even thou, not at liberty
move?
Shall serpents still struggle to bind thee, while thou
from above

[1] Caesaris (or "Czaris"), written in 1831, on the occasion of
the suppression of the Polish insurrection and dedicated
to the sword of Romarino, the Italian adventurer in
Polish service.

Art turning the helm of the spheres that are heeling
in Space?
Shall thy bolts by humanity's tears be deflected, and
falter and flag?
Shall a sigh stop the storm of thy purpose almighty,
the world in its race,
As a lion is turned by a rag?
O brothers who perish, sing glory to God while we die!

Then worship, O race that survives us, the hand that
bestows,
In the bolt of the lightning it launches, a shoot of
life's rose.
We saw not the hand, when with largesse of blessings
it came;
But only while swinging its hammer to crush us, or
raised in its might,
Or grasping its thunders, the neck of the haughty
transgressor to smite
With a horror of darkness and flame.
O brothers who perish, sing glory to God while we die!

THE DIRGE OF THE HARP OF ERIN [1]
(Transl. by J. Bithell.)

ERIN, I know where floating on Ocean's bosom thou
liest.
Past thee the sailor veers, suspecting thy sea-hidden
valley,

[1] Erins Klageharpe. Prefixed to the first edition of Spaniolen
(The Spaniard), 1833, which was dedicated to "an old
grey republican, the son of unhappy Erin, Robert Major."

Though he beholds it not, behind jagged mountains
of billows.
Only the eagle and Fitzgerald's soul see thee whole
from the heavens,
Like to a dark green lotus-leaf floating and cradling
thy snowy
Swan-flower: O'Connell's castle, shining far o'er the
sea-foam.
But God and angels see that the demon of Europe has
settled,
Holy lotus, upon thee. The tempest mows down like
cornfields
Pious towers of thy towns, but blows him not into
the ocean.
O that thy stalk could be freed! Then thou shouldst
drift to the fortunate
Realm of the new world beyond, where Liberty
mightily throning
From thee the demon should drive and gently, her-
self, on thee settle.

Ah! but under the sea to Albion Erin is fettered!
Sinister, lofty, and swift, like a water-spout in its fury,
Falcons strange flashing round him, the demon dark
hovers over
Erin's evergreen sea in the sea, oasis in Ocean.

But over prostrate Erin spirits sublime hover proudly.
Shannon groans, but hark! from the clouds overhead
peals forth music.
Borne by the souls of the Saved who lived and perish-
ed for Erin,

Hovers a heavenly harp, and the spirits gaze down
                    where their bleaching
Bones strew the plain, the while, like lifting, upleaping
                    billows
Rising in rivalry they in turn sweep the resonant
                    harpstrings.
Wistful melodies dirge the sorrow of Erin—the demon
Shrinks, and the falcons, fluttered, fly screeching
                    under his pinions.
For Erin's woe stirs the world to its deeps, and all
                    the world's races
Cry in anguish: O help! lest the foam-girded paradise
                    perish!

AT THE CONFIRMATION OF A SAILORBOY
RETURNING TO HIS ANCESTRAL FARM [1]

(Transl. by G. M. Gathorne-Hardy.)

'Tis a noble task to plough
Ocean blue or dark-brown mould,
Cleanly turn with share or prow
Sea above or earth below:
In them both lies hidden gold.

Yet within thee thunderous leaps
A still darker, stormier sea,
Where thy guardian angel sleeps,
Like a mermaid fair, who keeps,
Prisoned deep, a hoard for thee.

[1] Ved en til sin Odel hjemvendende Sjøguts Confirmation.
1833.

In thy breast I know a field
Planted with the blooms of Heaven:
Brighter gold is there concealed
Than the sceptre monarchs wield,
Or the glittering star at even.

Waves which in thy bosom flow
Must be cloven to the base!
O, that heart-soil rather plough
—Where unfading blossoms grow—
Than the soil thy footsteps pace.

Yea! thy thought the breast's wild sea,
Coulter-keen, must furrow deep;
Till, to catch the stars for thee,
Forth, on shining wings spread free,
Shall thy captive angel sweep.

Drive, like share of steel, thine eye
Through thy heart-soil turned and torn,
Until thence shall rise on high
Flowers whose glories may outvie
Gold of sceptre, star or corn.

TO A YOUNG POET [1]
(Transl. by I. Grøndahl.)

BARD! Look *thou* not behind thee,
Not toward the rune-covered stones,
Not toward the grave-mound, barbaric days hiding!
Those shields, let them lie! Let them moulder, those
bones!

[1] Til en ung Digter. From Digte 2den Ring, 1833.

Archaeologist ants, let *them* creep about on that
mound;
Them a handful of dust will—like snuff an old woman—
Inspire to tell tales that incredible sound.

A greater hero see than those 'neath thy soil at rest.
His heel treads a dragon, a serpent his belt is,
And hard-hewing eagles his helmet crest.

Towering, the hero treads the rank dragon into its
grave.
His heart swells, and straightway the serpent is
shattered,
That around it did roll like a great rolling wave.

The eagles, gulls of the ether blue deep, he shakes them
amain,
Like a storm-swayed mast; then like mist from the
mountain,
From his brow they exhausted sink into the main.

In his strife he is speeding over a great open sea;
Dimly distant as stars other white sails surround him:
There heroes with dragons are fighting as he.

Forwards over an e'er dawning blue the hissing bows
glide.
Blood-stained the ankle; the forehead high-lifted,
bright shining—
Not hawks, Heav'nly spirits upon it will ride.

Happy the hero shall rest in his ship, deep in a mound;
But he lives there, yea lives, 'neath its roof decked
with violets,
And his name aye in songs of the spirits shall sound.

Bard! That mound shalt thou praise!
Dost thou not see its fair crest?
See'st not the glittering shield on its summit?
The tall, waving lilies that shine on its breast?

See'st not the hero fainting under the heavens, alone?
Nor the fierce, crownèd eagles that daring do seat
them,
Where spirits have chosen their temple and throne?

Did not snake-chained Humanity up from the dust
rise at last?—
Shake the serpents from off it, like the aspen its dead
leaves?—
A dull-rattling crown was each link that it cast.

A Voice:
Woe! The black snake is hanging yet at its foot like
a bolt!
See it yawning wide in the Vatican portals—
Its crown as the dome does the heavens assault.

Woe! Caesarian eagles are sitting yet on its brow!
Thro' the eyes to the brain they are hacking; tears only
In the empty eye-hollows are glistening now.

Woe! Long, uniformed ranks are winding, like serpents
steel-grey,
Round Humanity's limbs their coils ever tighter;
Every heart that dare beat they would stifle and slay.

The First Voice:
Bard! In heavens where Time has not entered with
measurèd pace,
The Seer with Victory dwells *ere* the battle,
And together with Hope soars in front of the race.

Flies not his vision ahead of all time, ahead of the
world?
The earth-ball behind rolls History's thunder—
The song of the Seer is the lightning forth-hurl'd.

On the dome of an unopened heaven rest thy stringèd
shield:
Soon it will become (like *these* heavens star-spangled)
A dew-glitt'ring mound on a century's field.

TO A PINE-TREE [1]
(Transl. by G. M. Gathorne-Hardy.)

Crowned, lofty scion of the pine
Whence Gothic architect's design
  Derived the grace and power
For churches planned in noblest style,
For Notre Dame's majestic pile,
Westminster Hall, or Münster's aisle,
  Or Pisa's leaning tower,—

[1] Til en Gran. From Digte 2den Ring, 1833.

In this dark valley laid aside,
Thou in thy grief thy crown of pride
    Dost in the clouds retire;
And far thy sombre glance has flown
To spires like pine-trees shaped in stone,
Perceiving, with a wistful groan,
    The portrait of thy sire.

The dastard axe awaits thy wood:
Like Hercules in dragon's blood,
    Thou in slow flames must die.
Yet perish proudly, pine, for know
Not all of Europe's skill can show
How such a pyramid may grow,
    So stately and so high.

Lament not thou, for many a heart,
Fit model for the loftiest art,
    Unknown in rags has pined;
There, brooding over work denied,
Some hero sits, some Tell untried;
A Byron, Plato, oft has died
    Unnoticed by mankind.

Yon Tell, for lack of tyrant foe,
Wars on the sparrow and the crow,
    And he whose brain could soar
To match the master-minstrel's lays—
Some trumpeter usurps his bays,
While on his rustic pipe he plays
    For alms from door to door.

Like theirs, my pine, obscurely placed,
Thy nobleness must run to waste,
   With lowly village spires—
Unworthy hovels—must contend,
Thou, Nature's temple! Fortune send
Thee first a Herostratic end,
   Immortalised in fires.

Thou stand'st a nobler temple there,
Thy dome the leaden clouds of air;
   No Lateran tapers fling
A beam so radiant and so fine
As those dew-spangled boughs of thine,
What sacred strains are so divine
   As those thy linnets sing?

Beneath what temple arches are
Such trophies of victorious war,
   So honourably won,
As are these pennons pearly bright,
Flecking thy darkest twigs with white,
Which spiders, in a hard-fought fight,
   Have stablished where they spun.

Dim spaces filled with incense fine,
A choir thou hast, a holy shrine,
   But ne'er an image there;
For sinless Nature, who did base
Thy root, to God speaks face to face,
Nor needs, like man, who fell from grace,
   To mediate her prayer.

Upon thine organ-pipes the storm
Its wild Te Deum can perform,
   So awful, yet so fair:
Join thou, my soul, that anthem's strain;—
"The house of God is Nature's fane;
No moss so small, no weed so plain,
   But builds a chapel there."

TO SYLVAN (A BOTANIST)[1]
(Transl. by G. M. Gathorne-Hardy.)

WHEN first we met, 'twas on the bound
That parts the quick and dead:
Where in pale strips upon the ground
The lingering snow was spread:
Of ice the last blue sparkle shone
By the first smile of green, whereon
A lark his music shed.

'Twixt life and death? 'Twas neither yet:
Mild spring nor winter cold.
Just at the equinox we met,
And at our handclasp woke to birth
A spark from the enkindled earth,
In the first coltsfoot's gold.

And like the tremulous smile, that wreathed
Pygmalion's sculptured stone,
(That dreamy smile, ere life yet breathed),

[1] Til Sylvan. (En Botaniker.) 1835.

On the bleak meadow quivering set
—Where first our casual footsteps met—
A modest windflower shone.

In the March violet, drooping lone,
—That tiny vault of sky—
With souls new blended into one
We joined in rapturous unison,
My Sylvan, you and I.

How lovely was the hour which drew
You first, my friend, to me!
It was no part of time, we knew
'Twas ours alone, and from it grew
A blest eternity.

Spring yields to summer. On the hill,
From earth's dark womb thrown up,
Sparks from her inner fires distil
To dandelion and tormentil,
And glowing buttercup.

But if a show so bright embowers
The chilly breast of earth,
Then surely, Sylvan, fairer flowers
We for ourselves may charm from ours,
In spiritual birth.

Here is a flower, of heavenly blue,
That from my soul has burst;
There, Sylvan, spring was born anew
The hour I met you first.

A VIKING'S HALL [1]
(Transl. by G. M. Gathorne-Hardy.)

PENT in a western valley's fold,
Like a berserk hemmed by foes,
A timbered hall did, in days of old,
Its sombre length expose.

A stranger's eye, as the eve grew late,
Marked naught but the dark cliffs round:
Low was the hall; the pitch-daubed gate
With no gold spire was crowned.

No vassals there in a steel-clad band
Keep watch o'er a lord asleep;
His shielded sentinel by the strand
Is the headland stern and steep.

Smoke from the hearth, like a risen ghost,
From the rooftree stealing black,
May serve for a wanderer's guiding post
To point to the hidden track.

When the door is opened, with eager cry
The hounds from the hearth-stone spring;
Well trained at the foeman's throat to fly
Who ventures a-foraying.

A sail in the corner moulders grey;
Keen bills in the beams bite fast:
The flickering flame in a fitful ray
From shields in the loft is cast.

[1] Et gammelnorskt Herresæde. 1835.

And bows from hooks on the wainscot hung
Their writhen arms spread wide;
With bundles of arrows, and cordage strung
From bear-gut and sinew dried.

Forth two gods, at the table's end,
Flash out as the pine-logs flare:
Thor and Odin their presence lend
To hallow the master's chair.

The gloom is cleft by a mimic sun,
The boss upon Odin's head;
But scarce a gleam through the shadows dun
From Thor's steel helm is shed.

The twinkling stars, through the open roof,
As into a well look down;
There smiles in spring from the peak aloof
The birch-tree's verdant crown.

A horn of gold on the table lies,
Sweet mead bedews its rim;
Vainly the night its lustre tries
With a murky veil to dim.

Gems full many and rich adorn—
Like stars in the evening heaven—
The hollow round of that golden horn,
Where the secret runes are graven.

The aged lord on a bearskin sleeps
In a corner; the long grey hair
O'er his wrinkled cheek and his bosom sweeps
Like a foaming torrent there.

The veteran's lips from that horn in sooth
To-night have been quaffing deep;
His soul is steeped in the dreams of youth
By the mead, as he lies asleep.

Helped he Harald in Hafursfjord
His golden ring of rings
From thirty crowns at a stroke of sword
To weld in the blood of kings?

Or did he refuse, like a Norseman brave,
To yield his ancestral gold,
Choose for his home the heaving wave,
And for shelter the mainsail's fold?

*

None can answer; for hall and race
Have perished in flame and bale;
The stone on the grave-mound holds no trace,
And saga forgets the tale.

WORKADAY LIFE [1]
(Transl. by I. Grøndahl, J. Bithell and G. M. Gathorne-Hardy.)

"This life is all so workaday"
Proud, purblind men will sadly say,
Who do not grasp life's meaning:
No great events its sameness break;

[1] Kun dagligdags er al din Dont. The conclusion of a Shrovetide sermon, 1836, preached in the chapel of Akershus Castle: "Grasp the spirit in the things, the meaning in the signs, the great in the small". Cf. "The Leaves of the Oak", p. 82.

Like Jordan to the silent lake
Its days are grave-ward flowing,
Nor deed nor record showing.

Yet was it not to Jordan's shore
The Saviour came, and made it. more
Than Nile was or Euphrates?
Well, even so, if Jesus may
Beside thy quiet life-stream stay,
Sweetly 'twill run, though slowly,
Bearing His image holy.

Each morning call Him! Void of fame
Day cannot dawn in such a name:
In that begin thy labour.
'Twill have, though without pomp it be,
Greatness enough for Him, who'll see
Its soul and essence, deeming
But naught the outward seeming.

IN MEMORIAM GREGERS FOUGNER LUNDH [1]

(Transl. by G. M. Gathorne-Hardy.)

Come when thou wilt, spirit beloved,
By night, by day, with dawn's first beams,
When first the drowsy leaves are moved,
   And flowers awake from dreams.

With dew-washed eyes their shoots perceive
(As thou in heaven) earth's beauties stay—
Though whelmed of late in flames of eve—
   More grand than yesterday.

[1] Professor of Law in the University at Christiania. Died from injuries sustained in a fire. 1836.

Then from its opening buds is borne
The hymn which listening fairies hear;
O hearken, thou, and bring one morn
   That music to my ear.

Come then, dear shade, whene'er thou wilt;
Yet not thy tortured flesh to show,
That trophy of thy courage, spilt
   In fiery overthrow.

But 'tis thy soul I fain would see,
The form of thy beloved mind,
For in that heart of constancy
   Beauty I still may find.

Unveil that shoulder which displays
The sturdiness that marked the man;
Firm as the hills it seems, yet sways
   Like feathers on the swan.

Nay, will not heaven, with mystic dye,
Obliterate each earthly trace,
Changing to smiles of victory
   The anguish in thy face?

Wrung not by earthly flame; there woke
Within thee fires more hotly fanned,
Kindled by those whose poisons choke
   The life-breath of our land. [1]

[1] Allusion to Swedish objections to the Norwegians' display
of national independence, e.g. the celebration of Constitu-
tion Day, 17th May.

7

Her joys are hushed, her banners shake
No more beneath their native skies;
She hides her malice like the snake,
Which sleeps, but never dies.

That was thy final pang; 'twas yet
The first that thousands here have known,
Since every day has dawned and set
    On trouble of its own.

Come when thou wilt, dear ghost, again,
With the first cock's night-piercing cry,
Or while in festal round I drain
    The toast of memory.

Thou in no sermon wilt dilate
On death or the caprice of fate;
But soul to soul wilt gently sigh
    A trusty friend's good-bye.

Now it is time, now it is night;
Lit by the lamp's dim rays I see
A jasmine bend its deathly white
    Illusion over me.

I look, but ah! my sleeping hound,
That bays in dreams, has sight more clear.
How empty midnight's hush profound,
    How foolish seems its fear!

Yet dost thou well so swift to fade,
Happy beyond as here of late:
Did not thy father's longing shade
    Beside Death's portal wait?

His spirit now with thine is one,
As in one blaze united flamed
Fires that subdued thy dust alone,
    But left thy soul untamed.

STATSBORGEREN TO COLLETT [1]
(Transl. by G. M. Gathorne-Hardy.)

I send you greeting, but to-day
"A bog" they call me, as before,
The folk who jostling push their way
    Through your opponent's door.

There was a toad, the clumsy brute,
Hopped from us once, to trouble you;
"A bog"—the title seems to suit,
    Well, I suppose it's true.

It is a bog: but round the pool
The wholesome, bitter buckbeans grow;
Like Venus bathing, fair and cool,
    The water-lilies show.

There stalks the heron proud, and holds
A speckled serpent in his bill,
While unimagined peace enfolds
    That wildness hushed and still.

---

[1] These verses allude to a personal attack on Jonas Collett
—member of the Constitutional assembly in 1814, and
later minister—which appeared in the paper, "Stats-
borgeren" (Le Citoyen), under an earlier editorship.

And round, in glittering reeds and high,
Their magic harps the fairies tune;
And there full many a song must die,
   Too fair to die so soon.

But now, since Fortune's shaft was lodged
   In Collett's agèd breast,
Triumph it is to be misjudged,
   And my complaints may rest.

THE LOVED ONE'S GRIEF [1]
(Transl. by J. Bithell.)

HATE me not, dearest, if above
All else, it is your grief I love.
Your visage casts forth such a light
As in Heaven's halls a statue might.
The sculpture of your face has ta'en
Its beauty from your spirit's pain.

O lofty spirit gloomed by care,
Let me in this thy sorrow share!
I love thy grief, because 'tis lit
By thy sweet spirit piercing it;
To me its delicate paleness speaks
As might a fainted angel's cheeks.

Dear grief, I love thee in my heart,
Because my Love herself thou art.
She dreams thee, feels thee, she alone
Congeals thy coolness as of stone.
She is a flower sensitive,
That only by thy dew can live.

[1] Den Elskedes Sorg. 1837.

IN THE DISSECTING ROOM [1]
(Transl. by J. Bithell.)

—YES, it is she! Bring here the light!
But stay before the steel glides bright
   Into this bosom bare!
The lamp's light glints cold as the gaze
Of them that wait behind its rays,
   And at this dead girl stare.

And the proud world, in her sad life,
Looked at her cold as this cold knife;
   And eyes of impudence tore,
Ere she was woman grown, the veil
Of golden visions fair and frail
   She in her poverty wore.

Something within my memory dreams—
A flower frore in ice it seems—
   This face is known to me.
A neighbour's child was my playmate,
Before I grew to man's estate—
   And this dead girl is she!

She lived in poverty, across
The street, a violet in moss.
   And gentlefolks would swear
It was indeed past crediting,
That from so base a birth should spring
   A maid so sweet and fair.

[1] Pigen paa Anatomikammeret. Feb. 1837.

Ah! many is the face I've known
That faded like a rose full blown.
　　Frail rosebud of the town,
Sin slimed it over like a green
Leaf over which a snail has been,
　　And fell fate tracked it down.

THE FIRST BUTTERFLY [1]
(Transl. by G. M. Gathorne-Hardy.)

FLY in, my butterfly, and gain
Warmth from the rose within the pane.
Trust not the sun, whose treacherous ray
But shines to lure thee and to slay.

The starling, that dejected sits
Upon the roof, has keener wits,
Nor deems that pallid gleam is grass.
Fly in, and hide behind the glass.

From icy prisms those hues are shed,
Not speedwell blue or clover red;
'Tis real snow that lines the fence,
No summer jessamine's pretence.

Come, little guest, such festal fare
As I can offer we will share.
Taste thou my earliest rose, and be
A second blossom on the tree.

[1] Den første Sommerfugl. 1837.

Fly in and settle on my pen,
Give it thy gentleness again.
So shall my fancies gather thence
The beauty of thine innocence.

Ah! Many a child of race divine
Finds no such open door as mine;
Yet like thee, flower of air, are some
Unhappy spirits who succumb.

Yet, little creature, come and hide
From earthly cold, and worldly pride.
I may be prouder yet, but fain
Love from such little ones would gain.

II.

The earliest butterfly? Well, come!
Make, if thou canst, my soul thy home,
From which so oft have flown away
Thoughts like to thee, with wings as gay.

Come, I am solitary now,
And idle in my thoughts as thou:
I do but watch the sun's bright ray
Among the wallflower leaves at play.

Through the wide pane, in lavish shower,
It squanders beams upon the flower,
Which obstinately darkens down
Their radiance to a broken brown.

Fly in, first butterfly, and rest;
Nay, fly then as your thoughts suggest.
Mine too, so oft on cold winds cast,
Shall beautify the dust at last.

III.

A butterfly? What lovelier thing
Could beauty to creation bring
Than those bright wings, with colours rife,
Those flowery petals kissed by life?

Like the last touch, supremely fine,
That perfects a complete design,
Thou, first when all was made, wast given
Life by the artist mind of heaven.

God's eyes o'er His creation swept,
Which still, as in a picture, slept;
He spake, " 'Tis good": thy shape then broke
First from the grass, and all things woke.

And still returning seasons bring
Thee, earliest messenger of spring,
To say that yet God's glance is bent
Upon His work, and is content.

IV.

Come then, first butterfly, and gain
Warmth from the rose within the pane;
Trust not the sun, that treacherous ray
But shines to lure thee and to slay.

Upon the wallflower's sheltering breast
In blissful dreams thou safe shalt rest;
Where oft my spirit lies, and seems
To draw its noblest thoughts from dreams.

Tomorrow mayest thou fly at will,
But come again with evening's chill:
'Tis winter's smile, that sunshine pale,
That warmth, the lull before the gale.

I too no heat in nature find;
Too cold the pulses of my kind;
My blood I spend, whate'er the cost,
Else had I perished in the frost.

Or no, not died, but shrunk and pined
To baser levels of the mind.
My soul had then grown mean to match;
My flowers of verse—a cabbage patch.

More genial warmth my dog can lend
From his brown eyes than any friend.
Though in a glance of hate I see
Fires that to anger kindle me.

But lesser things more fervent glow:
The first green shoots that spring can show,
The scarlet on an insect's wing
To livelier beat my pulse can bring.

Come, butterfly, I know the thing
You pine for is a milder spring:
Here you shall find it; all who would
May have it, who are understood.

One day for me in yonder blue
A friendly window opens too,
When, though no snow be on my brow,
Too cold for me the seasons grow.

And there beyond shall blossom bright
A rose of spirit and of light:
Where God shall grant repose to me,
Who gave my earliest rose to thee.

JOY IN NATURE [1]
(Transl. by J. Bithell.)

No flower is fairer than a smile unfolding
    To see the flower so fair.
The flower knows its Lord's child gazing there
By the same smile that lit His face beholding,
    On the seventh day, that all His work was good.
It feels it, as the loved one feels her lover's
Pride and enchantment thrilling through her blood.
It feels it . . . Has the young rose eyes?
For lo! its flames uprise!
The bud has oped its breast, as though
The smile's warm blessing made it gleam and glow,
As though from out its cheeks, rejoicing red,
The sunshine of all Paradise were shed!

Glæde i Naturen. 1837.

THE FIRST TIME
Prologue to «The Campbells». [1]
(Transl. by G. M. Gathorne-Hardy.)

THE "first appearance"! How it brings
A pride of place to common things.
Brief is its life, a flash, no more,
The moment ends, and all is o'er.

To humblest herbs such festal days
Are granted, for we chiefly praise,
When first their tender blades appear,
The glories of the wakening year.

The richest mines their treasures owe
To pioneers of long ago,
When elfin hammers worked amain
To fill the rock with lode and vein.

Had but the rose a soul, she would
Desire to be once more a bud,
When first it blushes on the tree;
She dies because this cannot be.

So kind is God, He gives to all
Their first success, however small,
When death is life, and life can rise
Upsoaring into Paradise.

[1] Den første Gang. Prolog til Campbellerne. Performed at
Christiania Theatre 24th Jan., 28th Jan. and 12th Feb.
1838. On the second occasion took place the "Campbell
battle", in which the Welhaven party was ousted.

Where ripe woods fall, He spreads indeed
The rainbow carpet of the mead,
But with a blasted waste repays
Wrong to the seedling's first essays.

Lo, where the ocean, calm and wide,
Has lulled to rest the heaving tide,
How yonder wave spontaneous grows,
And, with the rest pursuing, flows.
That is its "first appearance." Fraught
It seems with purpose and with thought,
As if an active heart were living
In that small ridge the breeze is driving.
That is its "first appearance." In it
Is all its life: it lasts a minute:
The next, however high it rise,
In senseless ruin breaks and dies.

How bleak the meadow lies and grey!
A night of soil, a cloud of clay.
Soon dandelions overspread it—
The weed that grows the more you tread it—
When first its pallid stalk broke through
The plant its "first appearance" knew,
Its triumph and its spring to boot,
A crown was carried in its shoot.
'Tis mown. It puffs in down away,—
(Sic transit mundi gloria),
The best of all its life was found
When first it sprouted from the ground.

From peak to peak how deep the dale!
A boundless channel for the gale.
There screams the eagle, old and grey,
To call her young across the way.
Beneath . . . what dizzy depths, where all
Is swallowed in a misty pall!
The water-fall, a dangling thread,
Flings its wild music overhead,
Nor can its loudest echoes reach
The height of that tremendous breach:
Yet flies the eaglet. This we may
Call flight indeed, this first essay.
This called for nerve; the blood must thrill
Along each pinion's utmost quill.
But afterwards, he safe may float
On spreading feathers, like a boat:
Above the world can tranquil sail,
As if supported by the gale.
The first strange flight, though not so high,
Was yet more splendid: *he* could fly.
He might have failed; but as he flew
He first his eagle birthright knew.

Why does the plaintive lover sigh?
Must love with "first appearance" die?
Nay, but *her* earliest kiss can thrill
The silver-bridegroom's memory still.
What can the painter find to praise
In sketches of his student days?
He treasures these, and tears intrude
Upon the outlines harsh and crude.

Why does the conquering hero boast
His earliest victory the most?
How oft the half-pay admiral's gaze
To his first flagship's picture strays!
High in our sovereign's hall behold
A sword-belt innocent of gold.
Sceptre and crown are not more glorious
Than this, he wore when first victorious.

The life that lets such moments come
To things inanimate and dumb
With equal tenderness consoles
The longings of our human souls.
For, like the rose's fancy fair,
The eaglet's flutter in the air,
The first green shoots when spring was new,
Our "first appearance" charms us too.
We none of us would lose, confess,
The memory of our first success;
Even for that later fame, which laid
That "first appearance" in the shade.
In greatness at the dawn there lies
A charm we proudly recognise;
Yet may such preference indicate
The modesty that stamps the great.
That deathless genius should display
A special fondness for the day
Of first beginnings,—here we find
The beauty of a noble mind.
Such zest for first occasions claims
For hope precedence o'er its aims:

Can vigour to its wings impart,
And fill with fire its eagle heart.

Soar then, my hope, though thou be naught
Beside the object of thy thought.
Wouldst thou from fatherland beguile
The tribute of a fleeting smile?
Then spread thy wings in trust, and try
Thy fellow Norsemen's charity.
Too kind are they the bud to break
Which would its "first appearance" make;
But, like the eagle on the height,
They watch the fledgling's faltering flight,
When first its venturous wings are tried,
However deep the gulf and wide.

A son, with hope, my country dear,
Now makes his "first appearance" here:
To-night he takes the plunge, that so
Your kindness and his debt may grow.

A BLANK SHEET [1]
(In a Friend's Album.)
(Transl. by G. M. Gathorne-Hardy.)

ONLY those whose wits are few,
Virgin page, belittle you;
Those who in your blankness see
But their own vacuity,
Which, unlike this paper, never

Et reent Blad Papir. (I en Vens Stambog.) 1838.

Can with fancies quaint or clever
By a witty pen be decked.

—With the same abashed respect
I regard it, as a maid,
Out of whom, by Nature's aid,
May be conjured by and by
Scions for posterity,
Which may turn out quite as well
Saints from heaven or fiends from hell,
Just as one can never know
What a virgin page may show.
Such a sheet, whose clear expanses
Might enshrine the loftiest fancies,
Better, sure, were left untouched
Than with drivelling nonsense smutched:
Overflowing, interlined
Frothings of a scribbler's mind,
On a page that else might be
Space for inspiration's flight,
Or as pure as chastity,
Like a seraph's plumage white—
Shame to do it such despite!
What a shame! I could have wept
Till my anger's flame had swept
Over life and sense and sight.

When I think it well may hap
That this trivial paper scrap,
Where my autograph is penned—
Treasured by some faithful friend,
Or by any casual gust

In a random corner thrust—
May survive me, lingering on
After I am dead and gone,
Then I shudder, quite appalled,
Just as if my rhymes were scrawled
On that very stone of all
In the church's whitewashed wall
Under which a hole one day
Will be dug to hide my clay.
Ah! How many years shall fleet
Ere the lashing rain shall lave
Off these foolish scrawls, that greet
Everyone who seeks my grave,
Or till age succeeding age
Cleanse the writing from the page:
When the last faint stroke grows pale,
Then shall recollection fail,
Then shall hate no longer rage.

Ah! Pure sheet, but ere I knew
I have desecrated you:
Inky lines like serpents gliding
All your purity are hiding,
And your brilliancy is gone
Like a mirror breathed upon;
Darkened and extinguished wholly
By my sigh of melancholy.

Thankless wretch! No leaf more chaste
Fluttered from the orchard spray;
Dear it was, as that I graced
With my very earliest lay;

Has no place in that profuse
Paper snowstorm of abuse
Which my neighbours' anger blind
Sweeps tempestuous through my mind,
Nor that hail of insults shed
By a hate grown day by day
Over my devoted head.

Thou, memorial page, didst claim
Nothing of me but my name;
Yet that this which you entreat
May include myself complete
'Tis preceded by these lines,
Where my soul, in counterfeit
Faithfully reflected, shines:
Since, if true what many attest,
Doggerel scribbled out of hand
Is what symbolises best

Henrik Arnold Wergeland.

IN THE OPEN AIR [1]
(Transl. by G. M. Gathorne-Hardy and I. Grøndahl.)

FLY, Spring-time fair, so light and gay,
Fly not with all my spite away!
I fain my anger would have given
One gloomy hour, by hail-storms riven.

In stormy bursts of hail and snow
Which laid the orchard's promise low,

[1] I det Grønne. 1838.

That hour would have to pass, when I
Might call my wrath to memory.

Now deep in the soft grass it lies,
Sweeter than love's near touch it dies.
As in warm jets of heart-blood living
My anger dies away forgiving.

If once, awakening, my scorn
Would start a chase and blow the horn,
My spleen was cured with laughter at
Orchestral frog and singing gnat.

Melts in the sun my grudge; that word
In plash of wave is never heard:
The shore's mild strains my ear beguile.
How well, sweet choir, you reconcile!

What fair and kindly greetings pass—
Would man but see!—from grass to grass.
Like withering straw he fades away;
Why miss the gladness of the May?

Itself a coloured sunbeam, shines
The basking adder, while it twines
About my ankle: go thou free,
Poor creeping thing that trusted me!

Of poison in this blissful minute
The snake's fang has no least drop in it.
Why should I mind the least those others,
That crawl about on my book-covers?

Come to the throstle's bridal meet!
Untutored is its song, but sweet;
Finely it mocks, from boughs apart,
The carping critic's rules of art.

O spring-time's sweet and fragrant air!
Believe that sylphs are breathing there;
But, blend not with that gentle breath
Your gloomy sigh—'tis charged with death.

And thou, bird-cherry tree, dost bend
Over my hut, a sheltering friend.
Never thy shade to anger yield,
Beneath thy boughs no grief may build.

The coming spring perhaps will strow
About my grave thy bloom of snow.
Or will its flowerets drop inside
The cup I kiss who have no bride?

Shake gaily off thy pearly crown,
Though on my grave it scatter down.
Some lover of so fair a scene
Make it a seat amid the green!

Maligner, seat you there, and more
Love Nature than you did before:
So may you comprehend at last
What influence o'er my strains she cast.

THE FIRST EMBRACE [1]
(Transl. by G. M. Gathorne-Hardy.)

COME to me, grief, on my bosom press,
Lest it should burst with joy's excess:
Heaven, with disaster, hell, with your pains,
Calm its commotion. For here awhile
   She has lain. Strike, foes!
Your shafts but soothe, when they pierce the veins
   Of a breast that glows
With the bliss of her thrill and her smile.

Sorrow and trouble have died away
Here, where her face in its loveliness lay.
Drowned she these in the deep of her eye?
Or sucked she their venom? I seemed to mark,
   On her smiling lips,
How a tremulous shadow of pain passed by:
   And the blue grew dark,
As her eyes' light found eclipse.

Innocent bride, thou hast joined afresh
Soul with earth, and with God the flesh.
When on my breast,—as pure and bright
As a saint's white robe, thy perfect brow
   Gently was lain,
Guilt with its tear-stains vanished quite,
   And my mind is now
Like a cleansed and lighted fane.

---

[1] Den første Omfavnelse. This and the following two poems
are from the "Poesier" addressed to his young wife, 1838.

My heart reflected an inward grace
From the sinless blush of thy maiden face:
To the waft of celestial wings was changed
The tress that wavered over me;
   And, O joy, my soul,
Demoniac once, from heaven estranged,
   Is, thanks to thee,
Darling, restored and whole.

I feel, where thy loving lips have pressed,
A glory shining within my breast,
And O, the paeans of love that burst,
At the touch of thy passionless, drowsy kiss.
   I was fired and manned,—
While my fancy drank with a burning thirst
   All the sweet of this,—
By a tender angel's hand.

Love, while you lay by my beating heart,
What burgeoning blossoms seemed to start!
Blossoms that lived, and dreamed, and thought.
Almond or apple was never so gay;
   So rich a stream
Of the sun's blood never the roses caught.
   My soul its clay
Left in a blissful dream.

Cold, dark spirit, hold thee apart,
Or blend with the blood that stirs my heart;
Let it flow supreme in its pulses still,

Let nerves aquiver their passion prove,
    And in ecstasy
Hark to the breast's tense chords athrill,
    Where, tranced in love,
She late at rest did lie.

THE LOVED ONE'S SLUMBER [1]
(Transl. by G. M. Gathorne-Hardy.)

SHE slumbers . . . Hush! She slumbers.
No more her gentle fingers respond to my pressure.
As weighted with snow-white roses the bough,
In sweet unconsciousness they are drooping.

What rapture, light as zephyr,
To dare to kiss the delicate rose-flush, her heart-beat
To every finger-tip pulses out,
Her clear, diaphanous, slender fingers.

Why throb ye so, my pulses,
Just now, when nothing seems such a crime as to
                                        wake her?
Now while the dearest daughter of Eve
In Paradise is allowed to hover?

Now wings her flight in Heaven
That lovely soul; may never an angel detain her!
For then would she slowly but surely fade,
Like monthly roses which shed their petals.

[1] Den Elskedes Slummer. From Poesier, 1838.

Then would the hues of beauty
Become Death's pallor ... Beautiful Death, I would
                                    pray thee,
Importune the greedy grave, till thy tomb,
Thou lovely corpse, was in my embraces.

Should loveliness be buried
In soil unmeet to thrive in? O happiest of lovers,
It thrives, it is breathing upon thy breast,
My heart the cradle that rocks its roses.

Not long delays in Heaven
The maiden's soul, it would but discover the blossoms
Whose pictured hues it longs to reflect
In those sweet radiant eyes tomorrow.

For, as her fancy changes,
They now with the hyacinth's rich violet darken,
And now with the borage's deepening blue,
And now forget-me-not's light they mirror.

How oft, as children peer for
The lily under the water, her eyes I gazed in!
How heavenly a springtide blossomed within:
So blue the violets bloomed in Eden.

Alas! My shoulder trembles,
Whereon her head is resting, so throb my pulses:
She dreams that she lies on a grassy mound,
And hears the elves who hammer within it.

More light than ever, flutter
Above her drooping eyelid the sportive visions:
For under its delicate milky enamel
Are hidden pearls that are meet for angels.

In fancies free and joyous
The spirit world in riotous butterfly legions
Its delicate bloom of glittering dust
Upon her slumbering lashes is shedding.

And yet this will be only
Drops in the sea; for under those arches are vaulted
Two heavens of deepest azure, pregnant with dreams
Still fairer, visions with hearts that ponder.

O like to her that slumbers
Must love itself appear in the nun on her deathbed,
Who fled from the world and danger of sin,
And now triumphant rises to Heaven.

Such is the face of beauty
In converse with angels; passion, thus art thou most
                                  sinless;
Thus charm is most charming, like to the lake
Which also slumbers when it is fairest.

Then deep the sun is mirrored,
Like this reflected Heaven on the face of the dreamer:
Then children at play will ruffle its calm,
Like smiles that wreathe the lips of the dreamer.

O that I saw that vision
Which, like a veiling cloud on the surface of Heaven,
Passed blushing over the maiden's cheek!
Her dreams are surely the songs of angels.

How lovely must her dream be!
For see, her lips are parted to pray it to linger,
And gently is raised the radiant net
Of eyebrows dark that would hold it prisoned.

She slumbers, still she slumbers.
O saints of Heaven, come ye and share my vigil!
For one day among your voices her voice
Surely my darling dreamer will mingle.

WITH A BOUQUET [1]
(Transl. by G. M. Gathorne-Hardy.)

He has no soul, who does not count
Nature an open book, nor knows
That the grey lichen on the mount
Can speak a language, like the rose.

Thou knowest it well, my love, canst find
The vision in the wildflower's bell,
Canst grasp the lily's voiceless mind,
And all the tales the rose can tell.

Let then thy pleasant fancy rove,
And on the summer blossoms light,
For her, ye flowers, your voices prove,
Who is herself a flower so bright.

[1] Med en Bouqvet. From Poesier, 1838.

From morning's reddening height on height
But roses like her cheek will start;
Where angels haunt the steeps of light
Are but pure lilies like her heart.

And only there where spreads the sky
In azure like a limpid well,
Such lovely dark-blue violets lie
As in her gentle eyes there dwell.

LIFE'S MUSIC
A Legend.[1]
(Transl. by J. Bithell.)

"Let there be light!" when God said first,
Life from life into being burst.

Trees like serpents twined and twisted;
Grass grew, billowing, where it listed.
The broad leaves of the palm-tree stirred
Up and down, like the wings of a bird—
Bird rooted, while the wing heaves.
As though they heard, the lilac's leaves
Upright stood, like a pricked ear.
The blood pulsed clear in the rose's cheek;
And flowers spoke beauty none could hear,
Like lips, that only in smiles can speak,
Like eyes, that with glances answer and call.

But all was lifeless, lifeless all!
Even the voice of the waves was hushed,
Like clouds in heaven they heavily rushed,

[1] Livets Musik. At a concert by the cellist Gehrman. 1839.

Jumbled in silent colloquies.
And the waterfall was not more loud
Than a cloud gliding over a cloud.

And lovely, but silent as marble is,
Adam and Eve in that Garden dwelt,
And could not speak what they thought **and felt**,
Save with lifted hand to lips or eyes.

But life within them shoots and darts;
More and more fiery beat their hearts.
And when life's longings highest rise,
They have no language save in sighs.

But O that buried deep in their breast,
With hearts of marble they had been blest!
Too dead and cold to throb and beat,
And tell them both that sin is sweet!

Their warm blood the way discovers—
But the Lord takes pity on the lovers:
Death they deserve, but God is kind—
He freezes the young sin in their mind . . .

Ere the bold thought broke into crime,
The Lord stayed it for all time;
But as a punishment he stayed
The motion that in all things played.
The life he quickens he stays at will—
All on earth is stopped and still . . .

In its deep bed the river is packed,
Like blue enamel, like firm crystal.
On the mountain's flank, a marble wall,
Rises the glittering cataract.
The bird flies, but as on lead;
The clouds are glaciers overhead;
In the vaulted forest there is no motion—
As in coral reefs weighed down by ocean.
Despairing eyes see but a pied
Glittering picture petrified.

At the dread curse the angels all
Down before the Lord God fall;
But never an angel dares entreat
That the earth be spared from judgment meet.

Stay!—Now the sea of radiance shakes,
About the Throne in billows playing,
And, cleaving the light of it, forth breaks
The voice of the Almighty saying:
"He the world from the curse shall free,
Who hath so great a love that he
Will leave the Halls of Heaven to live
For ever with Adam I then forgive."

But none speaks forth. For the first time now
Shame mantles an angel's brow;
Offering himself for earth's pain, none
Owns a heart that love has won.

The angels all, by fear surprised,
Sink their pinions paralysed.
Even Mercy, that angel tender,
No succour save of tears can render.

Then a voice rang, as though a star
Were hailing a brother set afar:
Harmony's voice—that angel he
On whose broad wings the Lord pourtrayed
The contours of the world He made,
Ere He commanded: Let life be!
"Heavenly brethren, now farewell!
I go to free earth from the spell;
Music through its wastes shall roll!
Sing into the life of earth, my soul!"

Out of the Halls of Heaven self-thrust,
The angel cleaves to earth's dust.
The first sound that rings above:
"Hallelujah! Lord of love!"
The leaves waft; the brook sings gay,
Running where wind-stirred rushes sway.
Stretched like a mighty silver string,
The waterfall on the mountain dark
Sounds organ music; and the lark
In the cloud his rapture is quivering;
The summer evening's sadness breaks
Forth from the full breast of the thrush;
And in the fir-tree's gloomèd hush,
Trembling, the violoncello wakes!

BEAUTIFUL CLOUDS [1]
(Transl. by G. M. Gathorne-Hardy.)

SEE, darling, how the departing day
On a scarlet pillow is laid away;
How the sun has set
In clouds of gold and of violet:
There, there at least,
In those fair lands afloat in the blue,
O there, it may be, fate's birthday promise may first
come true,
And I, your love, be installed a priest.

That beam which darts in the air aloof
Is the church spire, that gold its roof;
That purple glow
Is a flowery meadow in bloom below;
Each dusky layer,
By sunbeams pierced, is a pinewood darkling,
That red—our home, you may see with gold every
casement sparkling;
This very day we might enter there.

There, sweetheart, soon you will find a way
To hang your lute on a sunset ray;
Fresh blooms will greet you
In every window, and smile to meet you:
On meads of flowers,
In playful frolic with one another,

[1] Smukke Skyer. 1839.

Are baby cherubs who cost no pangs to an earthly
                                        mother,—
Your heart will whisper that one is ours.

Around us, darling, in shady groves,
A blest community lives and moves:
Enthralled they trace
My lore interpreted in your face;
In an eager band
They are thronging to kiss your garment's hem
About you, dearest, when home from church through
                                    the midst of them
We wander, both of us, hand in hand.

From "JAN VAN HUYSUM'S FLOWER-PIECE"[1]
(Transl. by G. M. Gathorne-Hardy.)

O ecstatic instant, when
All my bliss was born again!
Clogged with too much joy art thou
To be borne away as soon
As those moments slight and grey,
Colourless and scant of sun,
Wafted on by Destiny's breath
O'er the wastes of life to death.
O most precious instant, now
Granted by a heavenly boon
To revisit me today.
Not so fickle as the rest

[1] Jan van Huysums Blomsterstykke. 1840.

Which in ordered sequence run,
Thou must wait, in rapture bound,
Till my heart a tongue has found,
Till its thought can be expressed;
Till it weary grows at last
Of its pulse's speechless leaping,
Till the sweet relief has passed
Which my spirit found in weeping;
While my lips exultant cry,
While new radiance lights my eye,
While strange broken speech is flung
—Yet as lovely as the unknown
Language of the blest on high—
From my stumbling stammering tongue,
Wild, as if my wits were flown.
'Tis as if my heart were filled
With a warm and gentle rain,
And the seat of all my pain,
That malignant stalactite
Which from grief's continuance grew,
Sorrow's baleful growth, which pressed
Hard as crystal on my breast,
Into bliss were melted quite,
And in these my tears were spilled
Over all the boundless earth;
Rolling round its hills the shroud
Of a vast, life-giving cloud,
Which descending warm and dark
Blessed it with its vital spark
To a sinless, glad re-birth,
Quickening the deep anew.

9

LET THERE BE LIGHT [1]
(Transl. by G. M. Gathorne-Hardy.)

Chorus.

"Fiat lux!" Through the ages yet sounds the decree
  Unto stars that are nameless and blind,
  To the uttermost darkness assigned.
All glory and praise to Thy kingdom and Thee,
  Master and Lord, Hallelujah!

Solo.

To the dark God's summons came,—
"*Fiat lux!*" Then first in flame
  Woke the dawn on high:
Then the wave along the shore
First in mirrored splendour bore
  The lovely sky.

Recitative.

By the deaf night God's voice was heard;
'Twas felt where crags in silence slept;
  Celestial chords were stirred,
And every wind its harp-string swept:
  Sprang the stars from depths of night;
  Stood the peak in jewelled light.

Solo.

"Let there be light!" What lived ere that command?
All in the womb of darkness lay entombed:
  Beneath the sea volcanoes boomed;

[1] Vord Lys! Cantata for a festival in honour of the invention of printing in Our Saviour's Church, Christiania, 24th June, 1840.

The mist in columns blindly fumed;
  Nor was the shore's first outline planned,—
Till from Jehovah, seated in the height,
  Burst streams of light.

Then hills afar were rolled, as easily
As master artists at a touch supply
Beauty complete; dales sank, from height to height
  The heaven unfurled its canopy;
The earth, its bride, it saw with eager bridegroom's
  And their betrothal ring between   [sight,
  Seven-hued upon the cloud was seen.

Quartet.

"Let there be light!" By life 'twas heard;
By light's warm glow the blood was stirred;
Awoke and gleamed Creation's eye.
The flower appeared in all her grace,
The hovering falcon for his chase
  The bounds did spy.
The bee in blossoms sank from sight,
Lilies in that first ray shone white,
Low in the dust the serpent glided:
Flaunted the butterfly her dress,
The insect's dawning consciousness
  Its pointing feelers guided.
The light's first morning joy possessed
With peaceful warmth the rose's breast,
  It woke the birds to singing;
A Hallelujah hushed but high
The eagle wrote across the sky,
  In strong gyrations winging.

Solo.

Lo! In the world of soul are heights displayed,
Whose peaks are bathed in waves of light above,
Whose every shadow is a laurel grove,
    Whose names are graved by Memory's blade:
Those demigods, who for life's order strove,
And gave thought wings, and truth its victory.
    With Moses' staff can Horeb vie?
    O what a Pelion
Glorious and grand in Solon's spirit shone!
    What Himalaya claims
A range like classic thought's illustrious names?

And in that world of soul are waters deep,
Great minds that brooded on their themes profound,
Whence roared, while torpid ages lay asleep,
Resistless torrents, spurning every bound.
The depths of Plato's wisdom who can sound?
Was Hellespont, by Hero's torch made bright,
Deep as the learning of the Stagirite?
    Are island-studded seas
Clear as the lucid soul of Socrates?
    Or has Scamander's bay
Lines lovely as her poet's soaring lay?
Or Euclid's pages, in what sea serene
Are sun and moon and stars so mirrored plain?
That world, as yet by Ocean only seen,
Was mapped already in Columbus' brain.
Nor ever murmured midst her plains the Rhine
So grand a song as Luther's voice divine.

Flow then together, mighty streams! Yet ye
Can flood the world with blessings not so bright
As Gutenberg's great genius. . . Oh, through thee,
Our master, light commanded first was light.
Upon the earth a glittering shower he threw
Of magic symbols, strange, inspired and new.

Chorus.

„*Fiat lux*!" God's voice was heard
By the armies of the soul;
Crowned with light's bright aureole,
   Forth they poured,
   Mighty Lord,
   At Thy word.
See earth's ruler proudly pace;
Shines not in his radiant face
   Light's command
   O'er the land?
As the streams asunder part,
Now there flows through every heart
   One great light divine.
Learning's hoard and sage's thought
Like the sun and stars are brought
   Free to each of us:
Free as wells amid the wastes
   Which the traveller tastes
      Art thou, Genius.
Diamonds, lamping in the mine,
Not so closely guard their fires
As their light the angel choirs
And our mortal hearts enshrine.

'Tis their call, by rule divine:
   Light's pure flood
   Is the blood
Of the spiritual vein,
Which not Death itself may drain;
   Through the tomb
   It shall come
   To its home.

          Recitative.

But such this light's divinity, it shines
Where still humanity benighted pines.
Can waves around the world as swift be stirred
   As thought?
What other voice like that of print has taught
   Light's word?
Through this once more there sounds that cry of
   "Let there be light!"   [might,—
"Be light!" Give heed to truth, give freedom flight!
   Each letter's metal tongue
   Praise to light's God has sung:
Our noble master's art is God's, His mighty voice has
   "Let there be light!"   [rung,—

TO THE SENDER OF THE BOUQUET [1]
(Transl. by G. M. Gathorne-Hardy.)

There is—there easily may be—
More glory, more divinity,
In kindly acts unknown, unnamed;
Thanks may be fairer, unproclaimed.

[1] Til den, Buketten kom fra. 1840.

How publish mine, who cannot know
What hands these lovely flowers bestow?
Nameless as are their perfumes rare
Which fade upon the empty air.

Well then, thou nameless gift, be thine
This modest link with the divine,
That as to God my thanks are given,
Breathed forth at random into Heaven.

Yet, if no wild caprice of fate,
But heavenly justice, rules our state,
Then will my meed of thanks be brought,
As it desires, to where it ought.

Were it upon a rose-leaf writ,
Did some rough torrent carry it,
Yet surely somewhere it were meet
The flood should wash it to thy feet.

No boisterous gale should ever dare
The blessing which I breathe to tear,
But rather to thy brows should waft,
Like veil of elfin handicraft.

Art young as are thy flowers? May he
Who comes to woo be true to thee!
Or has he come? Then may the fire
Of this blush-rose his love inspire!

May all thy listening ear receives
On passion-kindling summer eves
As wonderful and lovely be
As this carnation's poesy.

What varied charms, what songs untold
The bud's unopened leaves enfold!
So may thy lover's silent tongue
Dream of new beauties to be sung.

Be thine, be his, romance that grows
Like to this many-petalled rose,
Compact of joys that know no care,
Of countless leaves, all sweet and fair.

Or if a mother thou, perchance,
Who long hast ended thy romance,
But hast, no less, a tender care
For a strange Ishmael to spare:

Thy children and their babes to thee
Bring gladness, as these flowers to me,
Who lack but this of joy complete—
Thy name I may not know to greet.

Wine on these petals I will throw,
O then, perchance, their blood will flow,
And their reviving lips proclaim,
Endowed with life, the donor's name.

From "THE LEAVES OF THE OAK." [1]
(Transl. by J. Bithell.)

BELIEVE, ye true believers,
    That the features of your face
Are carved by the Hand that poises
    Sun and stars in their place.

[1] Egebladene. 1840.

And the grasses here that billow—
  Believe with a faithful mind!—
Are greeted by billowing grasses
  Answering their kind.

Three yards down in the darkness,
  In mossed and clammy clay,
The gates of light spring open,
  And dead eyes see the day.
But why must the quick be waiting,
  When simple piety
Can hear sharp as an angel,
  And like a cherub see?

Look closely, ye shall have vision
  Of great things in the small;
Thoughts divine wing heavenwards
  From grasses withering all.
Their yellowing is a token;
  And on the fallen leaf
Ye find the moral spoken
  That summer's joy is brief.

Hear! Hear the trumpets pealing,
  When corn is bent full-eared!
Weird runes run in the wrinkles
  Of ancient trees and seared.
Straw has sung ere the mowing;
  And mosses' elk-grey skin
Hands divine have moulded,
  And moulded beauty in.

O poor is he of spirit,
  With fancies never blest,
Who knows not of the beating
  Of a pulse in the flower's breast.
That leaves delighted converse,
  His poor soul never knew . . .
Hark! a thousand mouths are speaking
  In the chattering avenue!

*

In tumbled rocks where the mountain
  Remembers with horror chill
The leap that it has sworn to,
  Yea, and swears to still,
An oak has driven his roots down—
  Here he is fain to stand—
He waves wild boughs o'er the ocean,
  Like the royal flag of the land!

Deep down in the scree the rowan
  Withers before it grows;
Already the hazel covers
  The grave of the faint primrose.
O that our ear were sharp now,
  Spiritual our belief,
Now we could hear the oak-tree
  Laughing from leaf to leaf!

For the long nights of September
  He spreads his branchèd dome;
Fog-white gnomes beneath him
  Spare the peasant's home.

Around the ridge of his acres
　Ramble the goblin folk,
But they only make the leaves grow
　On the strong boughs of the oak.

His crown the nights of autumn
　Have coloured with dark strength;
And the wild wet gales have hardened
　And nerved his great boughs' length.
Dark-bronzed how they glitter,
　Immortal all his leaves!
Like the crown exulting Victory
　For the bust of Caesar weaves!

THE POWER OF TRUTH [1]
(Transl. by G. M. Gathorne-Hardy.)

STONE to bruise a Stephen's brow,
Lie at odds with truth, art thou!
Blow as impotent as foul
Aimed at an immortal soul.
See the victor's aureole shed
Glory round his bleeding head.

Falsehood's triumph soon is past;
Every word of truth shall last.
As a kerchief's touch can throw
From the crag the hurtling snow,
So a word outspoken may
Whelm with truth a world astray.

[1] Efter Tidens Leilighed. 1841.

No mere whisper hushed and still:
Friends of truth must more than will.
Be thyself in part and whole,
That is victory's art, my soul!
Like Saint Stephen, all alone
Must thou stand and face the stone.

MYSELF [1]
(Transl. by I. Grøndahl.)

I in bad spirits, did you say? I, who need only a glimpse
of the sun
To break out into loud laughter from a joy I cannot
explain?

When I smell a green leaf, dazed I forget poverty,
riches, friends and foes.

My cat rubbing against my cheek smoothens all heart-
sores.
Into my dog's eye I lower my sorrows as in a deep well.

My ivy has grown. Out of my window it has borne on
its broad leaves
All the memories I do not care to keep.

The first spring rain will fall on the leaves and wipe out
some faithless names.
They will fall down with the drops and poison the
burrows of the earth-worm.

[1] Mig selv. These lines were written in reply to an editorial
article in "Morgenbladet", which had declared that "Mr.
Wergeland is angry and in bad spirits." March, 1841.

I who read rapture in each petal of the hundred-leaved
        rose, that gift of spring—
Me should a wretched rag cause to quench one second
        with vexation?

That would be like killing sky-blue and rose-coloured
        butterflies.
Such crime, verily, my heart recoils from.

It would be like strewing ashes on my head which is
        not yet grey,
And throwing away the diamonds of sparkling seconds
        which Time yet sows thereon.

Come on, journalists! Sharpen your fox's claws on
        the rock!
You only tear off flowers and a little moss for a soft
        grave.

Like the insect's sting in the mussel, insults breed
        pearls only in my heart.
They shall one day adorn the diadem of my spirit.

I hate? When a bird flies over my head my hate is a
        thousand cubits hence,
It melts away with the snow, it passes with the first
        waves from the shore and far out to sea.

But why should not my veins be wroth?
Rob not the landscape of its rushing streams!
Right honourable osiers, permit the brook to foam
        when it runs among boulders!

I love not blue sky everlasting, as I detest stupid
staring eyes.
Have I no heaven because it is full of drifting clouds,
fairylands of the sun?

And if I had none—is not God's great and glorious
enough?
Complain not under the stars of the lack of bright
spots in your life!

Ha! Are they not twinkling as if they would speak
to you?

How Venus sparkles to-night! Have the heavens also
spring?
Now the stars have shone all through the winter;
now they rest and rejoice. Hallelujah!

What riches for a mortal!
My soul rejoices in heaven's joy of spring, and shall
take part in that of the earth.
It sparkles stronger than the vernal stars, and it will
soon open with the flowers.

Glorious Evening Star! I uncover my head.
A crystal bath upon it falls thy sheen.
There is kinship between the soul and the stars.
It steps in the starlight outside the curtain of the face,
whose folds have disappeared.

The rays cover my soul with a calmness like that of
alabaster.
Like a bust it stands within me. Gaze into its features!

Now they are as you would have them. The scornful
ones are laid.
My soul has but the mild smile of a corpse. Are you
still afraid?

The rascal! The bust has a laughing heart beneath
its calm.
Alas for your feeble fingers: you cannot get hold of
that.

THE SOUTH SEA TRADER [1]
(Transl. by I. Grøndahl.)

FORTUNATE ship which leaves this country! If I am
to give you a wish on the way it is not "A happy
voyage," but that you may leave it for ever. Ah!
my wish is heavy; it may weigh you down and thus
be fulfilled.

Fortunate ship! Your pennants laugh, your full,
bosomed sails are like a flock of jubilant swans, whose
banishment to the North Pole is ended, and who can
now return to the palm-girt seas.

How your breast is heaving as if there were a soul
within it, and you rejoiced in the journey towards
your destination: the warm green shores which I seem
to have seen in my childhood's dreams!

[1] Sydsøseileren. 1841. Like the preceding piece, this and
the two following ones were offered by the author as
"subjects for verse-makers."

Or was I ever there *before?* Sure it is that thither was also my destination. But do not believe that one destiny rules the world. They shatter each other like meeting arrows, they devour and are devoured like the monsters in the drop of water, they fight and slay each other for the sake of power as men do.

My birth must have been a shipwreck amongst these wild and barren rocks. Woe is me! When at last I can leave them I shall have no lip for the sweet fruits in my soul's native country, no foot to print on its springy fragrant green, no arms for the slim brown maidens to shake down the oranges over them with!

Yet hasten, days, and make my head white like yon dwindling sail! Then death's sickle will cut the last rope, and I shall follow. For Heaven is where we long to, and Hell is whence we long.

Der Geächtete.

THE ROMANCE OF THE SNOWDROP [1]
(Transl. by I. Grøndahl.)

ALAS, can flowers also become insane? With what a sickly pale smile does the Snowdrop stand there on her little green spot in the midst of the snow!
"I am waiting for the Rose, my suitor, the son of
summer.
He has set me tryst here. I could not wait.
I have come too early; but he will come."

[1] Sneklokkens Roman. 1841.

"Poor little one! You must have dreamt it under the snow-sheet. He will not come. He is the rich son of summer, but you the daughter of poor winter."

"So is it; and yet my heart tells me that he will come. He has gold and velvet for both of us. He spoke to me and mentioned this spot."

For three days the Snowdrop waited, trembling in the ice-cold wind. But she did not feel it any more than did the Juniper, for all the time she thought: "Now he will come and clasp me to his glowing heart!" On the fourth day her head bent, for her hope began to flag; on the fifth a grey pallor spread over her cheeks, for doubt began to gnaw at her heart; on the sixth none could recognize the fair one; for she withered away rapidly under the thought that she was now in any case too ugly to be loved by the Rose; and on the seventh she was no more, for her heart had broken with her faith in her beloved.

Rest sweetly, pretty Snowdrop! Your story is that of so many a poor girl: simple but of sufficient weight to crush a heart and an existence.

At midsummer the Rose will arrive like a knight clad in gold and velvet. He knows nothing, but would laugh if he heard the story of the Snowdrop and tell it to the Dahlias and the Narcissi and to his bride, the royal Lily.

But, see, every spring the Snowdrop is back again on the spot. Did she once blush with life before the Rose deceived her,—or she perchance deceived herself with the fancy of his love,—and is the pale one whom I talked with, and whom I saw vanish, nothing but her ghost, every year living through again the story of her unhappy passion?

THE HISTORIAN MUNTHE'S BLACK CAT[1]

(Transl. by I. Grøndahl.)

O wonderful, glorious black cat, whence came you, light-fleeting like a mist, softly as if you would confide a secret to me? Yes! the sad one that your master has left you. An Oriental would call you the diamond of Night, an unspoiled heathen would worship you as a demon disguised; but I believe that you are in very truth a Fairy, transformed into a cat by some more cunning, jealous rival,—or a Princess from a distant land, changed into what you seem to be thro' some treachery of love.

[1] Historikeren Munthes sorte Kat. 1841. Mr. Laurence Housman, after reading these lines, remarks: "The last sentence I find a bit unsatisfactory and hazy in meaning. If I ask the cat to rub against my brow it must be to electrify my spirit; or do you want "electrify" to mean "Pass the magnetic current of his spirit to mine?" It doesn't properly carry that meaning." The objection is natural, but the obscurity belongs to the original, which has been faithfully rendered. Munthe's cat, by rubbing against Wergeland his friend, will create electricity wherewith to recharge the spirit of the historian. — G. M. G.-H.

The bride's gloves are not whiter or softer than your paws; the maiden's hand is not more innocent; for, should there once have been blood on them—who then can compute what the roses have shed to adorn the beauty? The topaz and the emerald shine not like your eyes, mirrors of translucent gold; a fresh-broken surface of coal is dim against your glittering blackness, sprinkled as with a shower of crushed pearls.

Ah! Thus Death steals about us on noiseless feet. Thus it strokes with treacherous kindness and mild as a breath the fairest cheeks; thus it follows us everywhere with staring eyes, in whose yellow flames a black core of desire is bounding like an unburnable little devil in the fire of Hell.

In the grave it must be as if there lies on the dead man's breast a cat, gazing in the gloom with phosphorescent look into the dim eye, searching his sinful secrets, heavy as a marble lion,—until they appear, one by one, without a sound, in the terrorstruck features.

One only the dead man keeps between his close-pressed lips; one only secret which he would guard from the terrible gaze, from the claws that are raking his entrails. It is that one about which he despairs, that one which he dare not reveal by one tremor of his features, lest the animal on his breast shall change into a serpent and push its head into his heart.

94

But at last, after a thousand years, in the moment when he is no longer able to retain his secret under the intolerable pressure, when it is on the point of betraying itself before the relentless gaze—at last, in that moment he gives vent to a shriek. The All-merciful hears it. Straight it is as tho' the heavens were rent in all directions under floods of inrushing light. The crushing monster flees. The interval of death is past. The spirit leaves its corpse and rises among the heavenly beings, swftly as the starlike drop from the floor of the fountain merges in the shining surface. Mountains could he carry in his flight.

Wonderful cat! You soften my heart by your gentle rubbing against my cheek. You sorrow. Your master has left you, but his friend has found you, like a dear household god among the ruins of a temple. Rub trustfully against my brow, as you did against his; for must you not then electrify his spirit with some of those sparks which it threw over the old dark scrolls of History?

MY WIFE [1]
(Transl. by G. M. Gathorne-Hardy.)

Ere, a modest maiden, thou,
Dearest, with my nuptial vow
Thine 'I will' didst whispering wed,
Thou wast like the harebell shy,
When it bows its lovely head
Out of sight in grasses high.

[1] Min Hustru. 1841.

Little chances, rarely sent,
Fleeting as a breath that dies,
Sure are God's unseen allies,
On his heavenly errands bent.
For 'twas such a mystery
Led me blind, my wife, to thee;
Wonderful, as is the sight
Of the bee's instinctive flight,
When among the fields it hovers:
Or the fluttering butterfly,
Which draws nigh,
And in play mid stones discovers
Just the flower
To adorn his bridal bower.

But now art thou, as my wife,
Like the bramble, ripening red,
Which has rooted fast and wed
To some savage peak its life.

Ah! What fancies haunt thee now
Of the precipice below?
Art thou fearful lest thou fall?
Art thou dizzy at the sight
Of thy cliff's sheer pathless wall?
Nay, the void
Measures but the summit's height;
And as if that crest enjoyed
Calm of sovereignty complete,
So the depths subservient meet,
Overawed, about its feet.

Or beholdest thou aghast
Ravens fell,
With discordant croakings past
Darkly sweep,
As these legions of the deep
Were tormented souls from hell?
See, thy rock
All their turmoil cannot shock,
Cannot stop—
Howsoever high their soaring—
Light from pouring
Tranquil on the mountain top.

There, on high, mid storm and strife,
Where the raven wheels and glooms,
Sweetly blooms
This, my blessed tree of life.
Here, beside a manly breast,
Where her gentle head reposes,
Smiling lies my love at rest,
Safe and happy as the bold
Shrub, the crannied stone encloses:
Where, (as if that refuge cold
Were the hard rock's very heart)
Where alone, with fostering art,
It has crumbled to make ready
For the thronging windflower's mirth,
For the gentian's hardy shoot,
For the saxifrage's white
Fairy rings, a root-hold steady:
So with these to intertwine

Mossy blankets soft and fine,
Close and warm,
Round about the bramble's root.

How must then the bush delight
In its throne twixt heaven and earth!
And how can this brow dismay thee,
With its storm-clouds racing by?
Since they vanish at thy charm,
Since their sullen wreaths obey thee,
Tamed by one sweet ray serene
From the sunshine of thine eye.

Let it pass, that cloudy pall,
Rolling like the ocean tide,
Let its rage on this wild brink,
Free and keen,
Rise again, again to fall,
Waste, like waves that break and sink
By their own fierce might betrayed.
For what else are clouds that hide
From our mortal eyes the sky
But the transitory shade
Which pertains to earthly strife's
Daily round, but not to life's
Dawning immortality!

What are worth the crags that lack
Precipices grim and black,
Girded by no ravens' flight,
Shrouded by no cloud-cap's night?

What were man to mastery born,
Did no baseness him beset?
What were he, unless his scorn
Soared above it higher yet?

Ah, but how
Were the cliff's stern steepness fair,
Did no sweet bush nestling there
In the sheltering cleft repose,
Safe, despite the gulf below?
Could I smile on all the woes
That betide me,
Wert not thou, dear wife, beside me?

From "THE SWALLOW"
(Transl. by G. M. Gathorne-Hardy.)

BLESSED, blessed is the being
Blessed, whether man or beast,
Who, (when dawn has tinged the east,
While above the darkling river
Still the soft white mists of night
As in pastime glide and quiver,
Ere along the orient height
Have the sun's cloud-legions ceased
Rearing purple tent by tent),
Has to God his greeting sent;
Earliest greeting, earliest sound
From the grateful life around.

[1] Svalen. 1841. "A Summer Morning Fairytale for Mothers who have lost Children, told to my Sister Augusta at Jelsö."

Wordless utterance, yet begetting
Language in the bud, a setting
For a glorious temple hymn:
  Tuneful measures
In its mute appeal it treasures,
Which entrance the cherubim.
  As enfolden
  With its golden
Lofty crest of plumes, the palm
  In the swelling
  Bud is dwelling,
In the first awakening cry
Of the creature's joy there lie
Lofty hymn, majestic psalm,
Mighty prayer,—a three-fold dower,
Rich in wonder-working power.

Pray then ere the sparrow waking
With his artless chirp shall win
Grace thou needest in thy sin;
Ere the aspen's leaf is quaking,
When the morning breezes stir,
Ere the nightly dews are shaking
From the spider's gossamer;
While its wealth of pearls illumes
Still the thistle's crown of plumes;
Ere the meadow harebells gay
Have as yet begun to sway,
Pealing for the hour of prime,
At a puff of wind, a chime

Which with keen attentive ears
The adoring angel hears,—
Where their silvery stamens swing
Deep beneath his hovering wing—
Over all the sounds that pass,
Sighing, from the wind-swept grass.

Then, it may be, will be given
An experience to thy soul,
Which shall culminate in Heaven:
Midst the rapturous sights that follow
Thine enchanted soul shall dwell,
While thine eye, its inward ray
At that instant flown away,
Shall be like an empty, hollow,
    Sunken well,
Whence the waters all have fled.
Whilst it seems that thou art sleeping,
Art bereft of sense and sight,
Then thy soul in angel's keeping,
In thy fancy's idle flight,
Through the misty valley slips;
And, as prayer escapes thy lips,
As its earliest word is said,
Straight a seraph with thee flies
Through the gates of Paradise;
And one instant of Salvation's
    Bliss shall pay
For thine early supplications
And thy loss of sleep that day.

For when down the vaulted skies
Stars that crown the darkness droop,
  Spirits stoop
Down with them, and by thy cot,
Mortal, hearken, speaking not,
Eager that from thence may rise—
Not from bird upon the tree—
Nature's glad doxology:
And that earliest prayer assist
With exultant melodies
To the Mercy throned above.
Yea, when ne'er a sound is heard
From the lips of men unfeeling,
Lifeless as their fast-closed eyes,
With a sad complaint they list
To the first notes of the bird
From the misty woodlands pealing.
Happy bird! His timely lay
Wins a charm from falcon's fray;
  Archer's shaft
In its flight but dew has quaffed,
Nothing but the foliage hitting
Under which the bird was sitting.
No securer o'er the church
Glitters high the golden ball,
Than the wakeful siskin's small
Shining breast of green and gold
From the summit of the birch,
While his joyous notes are rolled
Boldly from his swelling throat,
  As 'twere armed

With a magic armour coat
Gainst the hawk, who from the high
  Fir-tree nigh,
Blinking, eyes his prey unharmed.

Early then thy Maker greet,
Lest the bird should thee defeat;
Lest the angels' verdict be
Thou art less devout than he;
Let thy thought to meet them fly
Ere the dawn has lit the sky,
Ere the wakeful skylark draws
With his music Heaven's applause.

Ere the wagtail's feet are set
On the alchemilla wet,
Ere the pearly dewdrops roll
From the lily's pendant bowl,
While the rose with thirsty lips
Still their icy coolness sips,
  Must thou raise
To thy Maker thanks and praise.

TO THE BONNIEST LASS IN TEVIOTDALE[1]
(Transl. by G. M. Gathorne-Hardy.)

Whisht! Her name I'll no be namin',
Hers, o' lasses a' the wale,
Sae the mair blithe een may glisten

[1] Til den venast Gjente i Hallingdal. From Langeleiken, a garland of verses in upland dialect, 1842.

'Mang the haughs o' Teviotdale;
An' the mair braw cheeks be blushin',
Like the rose in simmer mead;
There's a routh o' weel-faured faces
Frae Caerlanrig doon tae Tweed.

Whaur'll ye fin' the canty lassie,
Thinks na in her benmost min'
She o' queans the lave surpasses,
Like the birk fornenst the pine?
—Or the gowd amang the siller—
Sure, she thinks, it canna be
Sic a roosin' rhyme's intendit
For anither lass but me!

She I mean has een that sparkle
Like the bluebell on the lea
Glintin' i' the dews o' mornin',
Teeth as white as milk tae see;
Dimples like the crinkled crannies
Whaur the rose's petals cling,
Voice as when in siller tassie
Tinklin' fa's a gowden ring.

Fair her hue as snawy mountain
Wi' the lowe o' mornin' red;
In a croun she wears her tresses,
Snoodit wi' a crimson braid;
Locks o' gowd like sunbeams shinin',

Syde as robe wad busk a queen,
Gin I were a wee-bit gowan
Yon's the place I'd chuse tae dee 'n.

Lichtsome as the wimplin' burnie,
Jimp she is as withy wand;
Wark? It gangs like fit-ba' fleein',
Neath her deft an' busy hand.
Frae her dainty fit the grasses
Rise again like springs o'steel:
Dancin'? Whaur's the lad o' mettle
Daurs tae match her i' the reel?

Aft she sings, wi' grace enchantin',
Frae a hert that's blithe an' gay;
Ye'd jalouse a fairy fiddle
Plantit in her bosom lay:
An' her melodies! The mavis
Minds na sic a wale o' tune;
Troth, I'd need be gleg at rhymin'
Ere ma roose wis fairly dune!

Had I wealth o' gowd an' siller,
I wad gie ma bonnie bride
Sic a croun o' rarest splendour
As wad sparkle far and wide:
But, sin' sangs are a' ma treasure,
Wha but she suld hae the hale,
She, the brichtest, bonniest lassie
That I saw in Teviotdale?

PARTED FRIENDS [1]

Henrik Wergeland to Ludvig Daa.
(Transl. by G. M. Gathorne-Hardy.)

FORLORN and broken-hearted,
Yet smiling to disguise
The pain that, since we parted,
Lives ever in my eyes,
I pray thee, come, my cherished,
My sworn familiar friend,
From all the thousands perished
I keep an hour to spend.

An hour to speak and ponder
On life's swift flowing stream,
Whose eddies dashed asunder
In foam our lovely dream:
Seek we the fall's high ledges,
Gaze on its whirling spray,
So friendship's easy pledges
Melt in blown froth away.

Stand by the brink and shiver;
Thou dar'st not look, where borne
Up from the roaring river
Echoes an oath forsworn.
Take heart! Aloft, the birches'
Gay banners flutter free:
Ah! Yonder by the church is
Where our next tryst will be.

[1] Fordums-Venner, Ballade. 1842.

Come, sit we in the meadow;
Its grass is brown and dead;
Say, does not this but shadow
The life our friendship led?
Like the spring grass it flourished,
It withered like the hay,
And every seed it nourished
The winds have shorn away.

Here on the hill-top tarry,
Where clouds are racing by;
Lo! two the breezes carry
Joined fast as you and I.
One instant serves for breaking
That brother-bond in twain;
So mutual forsaking
Was all our friendship's gain.

Come, sit thou down beside me,
Come, to my bosom press;
Learn there what woes betide me,
As I thy happiness:
Once in its inmost chamber
Thy place, of right, was set;
Alas! that I remember,
Alas! thou couldst forget!

Come, let us turn our faces
Where hangs the headlong steep,
Cling close in fond embraces,
And then, my friend, one leap!

There rest, by deeps enshaded,
Two lives that once were one:—
Ah! had my memories faded,
Or thine less swiftly gone!

THE ARMY OF TRUTH [1]
(Transl. by G. M. Gathorne-Hardy.)

WORDS, the world so light ensteemeth?
  Lower yet,
Words in poet's stanza set!
O how frail your power seemeth,
  To be fighting
For the truth mankind is slighting.

Truth should come with thunder pealing,
  Flashing levin:
To her succour sent from Heaven,
Angel hosts their cohorts wheeling,
  Wide extended,
Should escort her advent splendid.

Ah! why comes she not, the exalted,
  Hither now?
With a helm about her brow,
Fashioned of the sky star-vaulted,
  Fiercer looming,
Swords her radiant pinions pluming?

[1] Sandhedens Armee. Introduction to Jøden ("The Jew"), 1842.

Why are not her white tents planted,
    Far and wide,
Gleaming on the mountain side?
Why are not her warriors granted,
    In their striving,
Mastery over life and living?

Bastioned night is steep for storming;
    Bigotry
Rests secure on columns high;
Like Egyptian serpents swarming,
    Round her temple,
Error's black-robed guards assemble.

Onward yet, brave words, undaunted,
    Howso few;
Earthly triumph has to you
By the God of light been granted,
    Who are serving
Truth, his child, with faith unswerving.

Forward, words, the truth's selected
    Hero band!
Soon in human hearts shall stand
Your victorious tents erected;
    Glory sweeping
Sunlit folds above your sleeping.

Forward, then, with fearless faces,
    Truth's firm line!
Yours shall be, by pledge divine,

Power no earthly might displaces;
    Death can never
Still thee, voice of truth, for ever.

Cease then, puny host, your quailing,
    Truth her cause
Through defeat to triumph draws:
Falsehood's desert heights assailing,
    See, your powers
Dissipate those phantom towers!

THE THREE [1]
(Transl. by I. Grøndahl.)

WHAT wonderful temples of human charity are not
the public hostels of the Orientals! Turks and
Bukhars have their caravanserais, the Persians their
khans, the Hindus their temple-like resting-places,
the Beduins and the wild Kabyles their inviolable
marabouts, and everyone without distinction is at
home in the Arab's tent. Had he been a richer man,
and had he not lived scattered over the desert, he
also would have built caravan-serails and khans for
the stranger, for those are nothing but an exalted
transformation of the tent of his fathers. It is the
same hospitality of the tent which has opened those
spacious stone-built halls in which the travelling Turk
binds his steed and feels well at ease, where the
Armenian takes in his camel, where the Jew or the

[1] De Tre. From Jøden ("The Jew"), 1842.

Nazarene finds room for his bundle and himself in the ever open hospitable cells.

Every religion has a mild and loving heart. These benevolent institutions are due to the one which we Christians believe to have the hardest heart. They are religious in their origins, whether they have been created at public or at private cost. The latter is often the case. The pious Mohammedan or Hindu bequeaths to these hostels as the Christian does to churches, convents and hospitals. It is *the whole* of humankind that he in his heart wishes to help when he builds such a hostel with gates open to the four corners of the world, or sinks a well in the desert, or leads a fresh fountain to the resting-place of the beasts. Also of them does he think the old, grim, bearded philanthropist whom Allah, Brahma, and the God of the Christians bless!

Somewhere beyond The Dead Sea there is in sun-scorched Syria a desert, which the infidels' charity has gone by—, not that it has not been discovered, but because Allah just at the journey's end has here given a natural caravan-serail in the shape of a gigan-tic plane-tree with room, shelter and fresh water for a whole caravan if needed. Chance brought together here one evening a Mohammedan, a Christian, and a Jew. The Mohammedan, a mollah or priest, had scarcely watered his horse, before a black spot on the horizon foretold a stranger's avrival. This was the Christian, a monk of the Order of The Holy Mount.

A mule carried him from Haleb to Jerusalem. "Salem aleikum!" said the mollah to the Nazarene, who returned his greeting in God's name. The stars were already glittering and the howl of the jackals was heard when the Jew, a rabbi from Damascus, unnoticed— for he came on foot—stepped on to the small plot of grass which the fountain had called forth under the plane-tree. In the days of King Solomon the fountain had also fostered this tree, and the latter had now in return as a good foster-son supported his foster-mother with his shade. Like mothers in their old age the motherly spring was still singing her lullaby. By this murmur the three travellers after friendly converse at last fell asleep, each in his root-hollow of the gigantic tree, and by the same murmur they woke up in the early dawn.

The desert lay beneath the mist within its horizon like a vast violet-blue ocean encircled by mountains covered with the glorious roses of Damascus. At one point in the east angels seemed to be busy putting up golden spears as for a tent. The travellers could see that the sun was on the point of rising. Something moved their hearts, their lips trembled. Each one of them wished to greet God in his way, but alas!— each was afraid of wounding the feelings of the other two. In course of their talk on the previous evening they had learned to respect each other; but now,— how could the mollah worship Allah aloud without disturbing the devotions of the Nazarene and the Jew, and likewise with the others. And still the need to give vent to their hearts' feeling in this supreme moment, and to thank the Highest for his protection in the paradisaic shelter they had enjoyed, was so great in each of them that their lips trembled. None, however, yet broke the silence. Quietly and hesitatingly the Mohammedan strapped the saddle on his horse without getting done with it. The monk showed no more expedition with his mule, the rabbi tied and tied his bundle. They were men with tact and feeling for each other and respect for the others' belief. Already thousands of glittering lances gleamed over the top of the rose-mountain. In the next moment the glorious image of the most High would appear, and the worshippers should remain silent? The lips of all three trembled; but no prayer, no hymn of praise sounded from them.

Then,—at the same moment, from the same branch of the plane-tree a bullfinch, a wagtail and a thrush begin their morning song. The clear trill of the bullfinch blended with the warbling of the other birds in a glorious, jubilant choir.

"Why do we tarry, brethren?" they all exclaimed. "Yes, with that which is on our lips?" said the Mollah, bending three times to the earth. "With the praise of Jehova, the Highest?" said the Rabbi, folding his hands across his breast. "Yes," said the Christian priest, making the sign of the cross,—"is this not a sign from Heaven that our praise also will be pleasing to the Lord, although our expression of it be differ-

ent?" And of a sudden, like the birds overhead,
they all three with a kindly glance to each other,
each in his way, burst out in a song of praise to the
Creator of them and of all things.

The Mollah sang:

    "Allah, Allah, great and good!
Evermore be Allah praisèd!
See his word in floods of light
From his paradise out-flowing.
See the Prophet's great commandment:
"Worship Allah, love thy neighbour!"
Over all the heavens scattered,
In the beams reflected, gently
Touching every tiny leaflet.

Ah, the distant palm is glowing
Like a Kaaba's vaulted dome!
   E'en the grass
Turns towards the East adoring;
And the fig-leaf's stainless hands,
Bathed in dewy baptism,
Lift themselves as if they would
Blend their humble, silent prayers
With Life's sounding shouts of joy:
Allah, Allah, evermore
Praise and glory without ending
Be to Him who for the worm seeks
Underneath the fern's cold frondage
With the mild warmth of His goodness,
For its need to satisfy,—

He who stretches
O'er the head of Earth's proud master
And o'er moment-living dust-mote
Love's enfolding, radiant arms—
Allah, Allah, thanks and praise!"

The Rabbi sang:

"To Jehovah praise and thanks!
Mercy are His sternest judgments.
See the cloud-hills, how they tremble!
Seraphs in the Orient soar . . .
See how all their wings are spreading.
Nearer, nearer they are coming
With loud cries of Hallelujah.

Gates of Eden wide are opened.
Cherubs wait to catch the sigh
That from Israel is rising.
Dire lament they glorify
To a choir of jubilation
    Which they bear in
Triumph to the ear of Grace,
Showing to the sorrow-stricken
    Victory's palms
O'er the throne of Peace extended.

Hallelujah! In the East
Mercy's rosary is broken:
All its beads, as rosebuds fair,
Cherubs o'er the hills are flinging.

Yonder is a Zion rising
Radiant in the heavens' blue.
Solomonic temple towers
Golden-columned on its summit.
 . . . See how glows with velvet purple
  The interior!
  Golden red
Seven-armed candelabrum
Like a constellation shines
From a gloom of deepening scarlet,
When it breaks the waves of darkness.
  Heaven above
Full of David's harps is hung.
Clangor of the stricken gold
From the morning cloud is bursting.
And on either side extended
Are along th' horizon's brow
Tents of the twelve tribes serenely
In the sunrise Canaan.[1]
  Dawn is in Jehovah's judgments;
And their night will soon be over.
  To the faithful
Shall Messiah yet be coming
Radiant from the heavens down."

And the Christian, the Nazarene, sang:
  "Thanks and praise to God almighty!
  See the morning light beginning—
  To proclaim his name afar!

[1] **A** liberty has here been taken in omitting the individual names of the tribes.

See the grass in tufted clusters
Bending down to Him who burdens
Also it with freshening dew.
For its holy water pure,
Sprinkled over grass and branches,
Sanctifies both grove and meadow
    As a holy temple-hanging,
Of the mountain makes an altar,
Where the shining ones adore.

Every stem that sunlit glistens,
Falls and rises o'er the plain,
Is a leaning-staff of Faith;
Every leaf a wingèd angel,
Every twig a cross of gold,
Wherewith all the air is swarming.
Every flower the sun has gilded
Is a cup by Mercy filled.
Heavenly love has tenderly
All its heart poured out into it,
Reached the chalice, overflowing,
To each guileless being, open
To the e'er-renewed ascension
Daily from the morning clouds,—
To the promise that is written
On the dew-besilvered meadow
Of a Love all-merciful,
Beaming forth in mildest radiance,
Flowing from the fullest cups
On our parched and darksome Earth,
    Of an Eden

Opened by the God of Mercy,
Round by rosy day-breaks girded,
  In whose clouds
Saints among the crowds of angels
With unfettered tongues are praising
The Unnameable's high name."

Thus it sounded simultaneously from the believers' breasts. They shook hands and now set out joyfully each in his direction through the desert: the Mollah journeyed toward Bagdad, the Monk toward Jerusalem, the Rabbi toward Damascus. But when they had got a little distance into the desert, it was as though the same thought stopped them and made them send a grateful glance back to the hospitable plane-tree, which now lay far away like a St. Helena in the ocean of air.

CHRISTMAS EVE [1]
(Transl. by I. Grøndahl.)

Who cannot call to mind a storm, a tempest
So fierce he thinks that Heaven no worse can send?
A tumult as tho' every soul, from Cain's
To the last one God doomed, escaped from Hell,
All cursed the Earth which made them give up
                           Heaven? . . .
A storm whose voice can never be forgot.
All thought: it must be sent because of *me;*
At me the thund'ring hurricane is aimed;

[1] Juleaftenen. From Jøden ("The Jew"), 1842.

My sin has become known unto the spirits . . .
A storm whose might can teach both priest and flock
To worship demons in that element
Whose crash the old man e'er from childhood hears . . .
A cloud-quake, a last judgment in the airs? . . .
A storm which shook the stout heart in its stronghold,
When thro' the uproar his own name was called
By spirits carried past him on the wind,
Whilst every tree-top like a raven screamed.
But in the rocks the raven hid; the wolf
His hunger tamed; nor ventured forth the fox.
Indoors no lights were lit, the dog let in . . .
In such a storm thou gettest prayers, God!

In such a storm—it was the Eve of Christmas—
When the tall night o'erstrode the cowering day—
Thro' Sweden's wilderness, the Tivèd forest,
An old Jew heavily was plodding onward—
Awaited in the villages on this side
From those beyond the forest, now for Christmas,
By maids full many longingly. His knapsack
Held brooches, ribbons, and what else was wanted
For coming days of Christmas and New Year.
Their longing knew suspense, but never fear;
For never had Old Jacob disappointed
Them any Christmas yet: he came as sure
As Christmas Eve itself.
In such a night . . .
'Hush! Was't again the tempest
Howling thro' branches? Was it not a cry? . . .
Ah, there again! Straightway Old Jacob stops,

And with strained sense listens a second time.
'Tis heard no more. For now the storm increases,
Thund'ring like cataract on him who's drowning.
He presses on. 'Hush! There again a sound!'
A sound that rose above the forests roaring.
'The false owl cries just like a little child.
Who in such weather would allow their child
To roam? The she-wolf wouldn't let her whelps!'

Again the old man weary totters onward.
Again it cries, and he can doubt no more:
This whirlwind which already over yonder
A winding snow-tower o'er the forest flings,
Has born a *word*, one single word, along.
At once he turns to whence he heard it come,
Working his way deeper into the forest,
Deeper into the snow, into the night,
Rearing like mountain-wall against his steps,
By instant-passing snow-gusts bleakly lighted,
As if the whole white forest were one horde
Of flying, whirling, veiléd ghosts and spirits,
Who howling rose each moment on his way;
On airy toe they spun, horribly growing—
And then were gone between the rooted trees.

Still the old man fights on against the tempest,
Advancing when it waxes; when it wanes—
Drawing its breath—he listens on his knees.
Anon he rises, penetrates the darkness,
As delving dwarf works thro' the pitchy mould.
. . . . No more he hears . . . . no more. The old Jew
                                        trembles,

Thinking that evil spirits him do fool,
And mumbles forth the prayers that he knows.
Then 't whines again, surely this time quite near.
His own call 'gainst the storm is carried back
Into his mouth. But there! look there! Ah, there,
Ten paces more! There something dark is moving
Upon the snow, as if the storm were jostling
A stump, a little loosened at the root.

'An arm! Jehovah! 'tis a child—but *dead!*'
Ah! Did the stars of heaven on this dark night,
When 'mongst them shone the Star of Bethlehem,
Think that no good on earth could e'er be done?
None of them saw this instant how Old Jacob,
As glad as tho' he had a treasure found,
Threw down at once his riches all, the knapsack;
Pulled off his narrow coat, carefully wrapped it
About the lost child's limbs; then bared his breast
And laid its cold, cold cheek up to it close,
Until it woke up from his own heart-beat.
Then up he sprang. But whither now? The storm
Has covered up his track. What did he care?
For in the thund'ring of the forest tree-tops
He heard the harps of David jubilant.
The stormy gusts seemed to him lofty cherubs,
Who, borne on snow-white wings, pointed the path;
And on his random, winding way he felt
The gentle strong pull of the Lord's own hand.

But how to find a house in the wild Tivéd
In such a night, when lights durst not be burnt?
Half-way across there was a lonely cottage,

Whose low roof could not be distinguished from
The snow, nor its black wall from the bare rock.
As by a miracle he was stopped by it.
There, utterly exhausted, sank he down;
And many a snow-spray flew ere he was able
To trail him with his burden to the door.
He gave a gentle knock—the child was sleeping.
Then he discovered he had lost his knapsack,
As he had nothing now at all to offer
The good poor people who would run to open
Their door with hospitable haste. Alas,
Full many a time he knocked, ere came the answer:
'In our Lord's name who's there on such a night?'
'It is Old Jacob. Don't you recognise me?
The old Jew?'
'*Jew!*' thereat cried terror-stricken
Together a man's and a woman's voice.
'Then keep outside! We nothing have to pay with.
Misfortune shouldst thou bring into our house,
This night when *He* was born thou slewest!'
'I?'
Yea, thy people—and that is the sin
Thro' thousand generations to be punished.'
'Alas! To-night the dog is let in!'
'Yes,
The dog, but no Jew in a Christian house.'

He heard no more. The cruel, cruel words
Cut thro' him keener than the winter wind,
And, stronger than the wind, they threw him down,
Down in the snow, bent o'er the slumbering child.

Then, as toward the window he did turn
His gaze—expecting that the white face might
Appear again—it seemed as tho' in down
He sank, and that delicious warmth flowed thro'
His veins, and that known beings, gently whisp'ring,
Like to the summer wind in grassy harp,
Flitted about his couch, till one of them
Said with raised, warning finger: 'Come! He sleeps!'
And in a bright-illumined hall beside
They disappeared; only the child remained,
Drawing the pillows ever closer round him,
Until it seemed to him he fell asleep.
The snow was softly burying the dead.

'O Jesus! There the Jew is sitting still!'
The man cried, as he looked out in the morning.
'Well, chase him then! Why, it is Christmas Day!'
Chimed in his wife. 'Look at the greedy Jew,
How hard he draws his bundle to his breast!'
'Importunate as ever with his ware,
Staring in at the window with fixed look,
As if *we* had the money for to buy.'
'I shouldn't mind seeing what he has got tho' . . .'
'All right, Jew, let us see!'

    The pair stepped out.
They saw the frozen gleam in the dead eyes.
More pale grew they than he, they cried in fear
And trembled with remorse. 'O Lord! O Lord!
What a misfortune this!' They raised him up;
The bundle followed; loosened next his coat.

There hung, with arms locked round the old Jew's neck,
Margretha, their own child, a corpse like him.
So swiftly strikes no lightning, darts no adder,
As pain and horror hit the couple home.
The snow was not so pale as was the father;
The storm did not wail louder than the mother.
'Oh, God has punished us! The storm has not,
But our own cruelty has killed our child!
In vain, alas!—as on our door he knocked—
We at the door of Mercy too shall knock
In vain' . . .

When through the forest road again was broken,
A man came from the farm where Gretha lived
(The little girl was quartered on a farmer's)
And whence she, as the Christmas bells were sounding,
Ere the storm came had wandered by herself
To see her parents dear on Christmas Eve.
He did not come to ask about the child,
But for the Jew, from all the village girls,
Whose hopes to go to church were now relayed
To New Year's Day—that is, if he were found.

There lay he, stretched a corpse before the fire.
His host, with gaze as frozen as the Jew's,
His body bent and crooked like the corpse,
Sat staring stiffly into the red embers,
And ever stirring, nourishing the fire,
To get it straightened out, and the hands folded.
In front of them Margretha's mother knelt,
Folding the stiff arms of her little one

Tighter and tighter round the dead man's neck.
'She does no more belong to us,' she sobbed,
'For he has bought our child by his own death.
We dare not now take little Gretha from him;
For she must beg for us of our Lord Jesus
His intercession; to His father
The poor Jew will complain . . .'

THE THISTLEDOWN-GATHERER [1]
(Transl. by I. Grøndahl.)

Noli desperare!

BEHOLD the vast field of thistles, a heaving ocean!
Like foam flies the down from the countless thous-
ands, which now, as though despairing at their
decline, pale retire into the deep. Fresh millions
reappear, rolling waves of flame before the wind.

Did not a greyhaired farmer sow the field, with
blessings, and make the sign of the cross over it?
Can curses grow from such a seed?

But see, out of the midst of the ocean appears the
head of a boy, like that of some one drowning! At
daybreak he went out to destroy his father's enemies,
the hosts with the proud cupreous thistle-heads, and
to pluck their down for his grandmother's pillow.

The little hero! How he mows and toils! He does
not seem to feel the rays of the ascending sun. They
must be cool beside his love. Insatiable do his eyes look

[1] Tidselskjægplukkeren. From Jøden ("The Jew"), 1842.

out over the heath. All its wealth of white down he
will plunder before it is evening and the old one seeks
for rest. The thorns are red with his blood. Onward
he longs, though he might at every step plant his
foot on the swollen coils of a snake in the dense
growth.

Already the midday sun has passed high over the
woods. The shadow has grown behind him like the
courage of the coward who finds that he is not
noticed; and still he sees the heath waving, full of
thistles, round his little clearing.

Alas, this too seems lost, like a whirl in the ocean.
The wind after noon has raised fresh thousands,
emerging like slaves bold with their numbers. His
hands sink down. The wind carries away most of
his harvest and sends a flying spray of thistledown
into his face.

Even so bootless is the labour of Charity to
vanquish suffering, which is abundant as the vices,
the bleaching of whose countless thistleheads it is,
so that the world of souls is like this heath, full of
flowering and withering millions. What wild growth
in these human souls! Let Death clear up this jungle!

The sorrows of others be as the flying thistledown,
at most worth the trouble of turning one's back on!
One angel only has remained faithful to man: the
wingless one of Indifference, with his dead eyes, fat

cheeks and complacent smile,—much as all angels, excepting those by Raphael, are depicted in the churches. He leads you past suffering with averted eyes as past an accursed pillar of salt. All your strength applied to lightening it would only be as a child's arms clasping the pillar in order to move it.

Lo, the heavens are high vaulted over the earth! Should their bliss be disturbed by the wail of its misery, the rattle of its follies? Rejoice in the beauty of the fields; but forget that ragged poverty ploughed them. Admire the rounded towers of the castles; but consider not that they are the helmets on the red heads of tyranny.

Ah, but will not Grandmother's love fill up the boy's ever-hungering bag, in which the down was to be gathered? Its riches have melted to the size of a snow-ball; but she will take the weeping boy to her heart and the down under her head, and declare that it has breathed heavenly sleep about her limbs.

Work on, therefore, with good courage, like the boy in the field of thistles! His eyes would reap the whole, although his arms all through the day have only swept a circle as wide as their own length. God does not count more than the will. When your cheek glows with righteous wrath other angels will come than that flopping amphibium, as in answer to a lighted beacon,—as though the flaming glance of sympathy were the secret sign between the souls and the celestial ones. The same shall come that in

Gethsemane wiped off the bloody sweat, and kneeling shall also the drops from your brow be collected, to become stars in the heaven where your spirit shall live, and whence the dark mounds of your workdays shall appear as distant vine-hills, glittering in the sunshine.

THE KING IS SUFFERING [1]
(Transl. by J. Bithell.)

O that these my tears that flow,
King, could bring you health's new glow!
   Make you young and lusty!
O that with my heart's warm blood
I your veins with health might flood—
   I would give it, trust me!

Like an elk or reindeer I
Over ringing space would fly,
   Every hindrance spurning;
To the bedside of my King
Help and healing I would bring,
   With devotion burning.

I would bathe your feet with red
Blood that my own heart had shed
   For my King's assuaging!
Then my last tears down should rain,
Balsam sweet! to cool the pain
   In your poor limbs raging.

[1] Kongen lider. 1844.

Swift work I of Death would make,
If he came then, like a snake
  On my hero stealing!
I would snatch that second fleet
That should sink him into sweet
  Slumber sound and healing.

Death's black shadow in the skies,
Where he like an eagle flies,
  He would see, awaking.
But at his bed's foot would ring
Through his room a broken string,
  Strained, alas! to breaking!

*

King, mark now the corpse they will
Bear from halls that festive fill,
  Bright with joy unbounded—
Norman was that heart of his,
Harp it was whose melodies
  To your honour sounded.

ON THE FUNERAL DAY OF
KING CARL JOHAN [1]
(Transl. by G. M. Gathorne-Hardy.)

In vain the shades of grave and chapel
Close on my monarch's resting-place;
Not e'en rapacious Death can grapple
His image from my heart's embrace.

[1] Paa Kong Carl Johans Begravelsesdag, 26th April 1844.

For in the depths of memory staying
There flashes yet his fearless eye;
Still smiles about his lips are playing,
Still gleams that brow, serene and high.

Ne'er on that sanctuary infringes
Corruption such as passes through
That door which groans upon its hinges
To mourning crowds a last adieu.
Within my heart's most secret chamber,
Embalmed in tears, my king shall lie;
Nor shall, while memory can remember,
Aught of his noble beauty die.

Though bells be hushed throughout the nation,
My faithful heart shall beat his knell,
So long as with its old pulsation
My blood shall fill each wonted cell.
Adorned in robes of scarlet splendid,
Her sables grief may cast away;
Yet in my heart shall ne'er be ended
For Carl Johan its mourning day.

As from no single blade is gleaming
The star's reflexion in the dew,
But mirrored in the field is streaming
In myriad sparkles towards the blue,
So wilt thou see reflected duly
In all the nation's souls as one
The image I have kept so truly,
But which I might not keep alone.

Yet will I measure my devotion
With all the love in all the State;
No rival in this pure emotion
My jealous heart shall tolerate.
This is my modest worth's adorning,
In all my grief my joy, my boast,
A flower to deck my robe of mourning,—
That I have loved my king the most.

LONGING FOR LAND [1]
(Transl. by I. Grøndahl.)

CAPTAIN, whither, whither—tell me!—
Goes the voyage without ending,
Coiled horizons as to quell me
Ever new about me bending?
While the brig in restless haste
Rushing sailed through many a hundred
By the selfsame mirage paced,—
While I wondered
Whether distance were defeated,
Visioned shores by waves were sundered
And into the air deleted . . .
Hundreds of horizons rounded,
Whereon shifting skies were founded,
And wherein my eye-nerves twain
With an unremitting strain
Crossing formed the constant centre . . .
Still we enter

[1] Længsel efter Land. From Den engelske Lods ("The English Pilot"), 1844.

More elusive sky-lines grey,
Which receding melt away,
Bounds deceptive as the bight
Startled serpent forms in flight
. . . Grey, alike, unto despair,—
While more cruelly could no raised
Burning-glass an insect follow
Than from out the heavens hollow
On our dwindling vessel blazed
Down the zenith's stolid glare.

THE APPEARANCE OF ENGLAND [1]
(Transl. by J. Bithell.)

CAPTAIN, O what can that be,
Which breaks forth and radiant shines,
Yonder where heaven's boundary lines
Flow together with the sea?
Can it be that yonder lies
Some fallen mountain of the skies?
—No cloud has so white a sheen!—
Can it be an iceberg, clean
Broken just and swathed in snow?
Can it be a foam-belt vast
By the wild Atlantic cast?
Haply charmèd swans in row,
Like an army's front, are massed,
  Ready ever, as they form,
At the first alarm to fly,

[1] From Den engelske Lods ("The English Pilot"), 1844.

As, when winds whirl up a storm,
Snow is scattered through the sky?
Is it the world's boundary string,
Mother-of-pearl all glittering
Like a silver belt, that bars
The eternal sailor's voyaging?
Or is it, wilderness unguessed,
Ocean's nursery of stars,
Which from its bosom, isles of light,
Break forth in the deep of night
And to realms unknown take flight?
Are they the bright halls of the blest
Angels yonder in the West,
Where, with God, they gaze into
All that wildering womb of blue,
Whence the stars to them rise up?
Glorious: as in an open eye,
  In whose cup
Tender, beauteous thoughts sublime
Rhythmic rise and kiss in rhyme!

THE SAILORS' SONG [1]

THAT which glitters in the west,
'Twixt the waves and cloud-banks over,
That is England, sun-caressed:
  See the cliffs of Dover!

---

[1] Det som skinner vester hist. Transl. by G. M. Gathorne-Hardy, with contributions by Mrs. Helen H. Porter and J. Bithell.

Life that English oak-woods waft
On the bracing breeze advances;
Revelling in that cordial draught,
   How the pennon dances!

Scents which Kentish fields impart
Sweetly now the air are filling:
Like his flag the seaman's heart
   Towards the land is thrilling.

England's bulwark, strongly bound
Pearly white cement, emerges:
Freedom has her stronghold found
   Mid the ocean surges.

God has built around her home
Massive walls and lofty towers,
Where it faces, o'er the foam
   Europe's envious powers.

Throne of marble westward seen,
Shakespeare's Cliff, far-famed in story,
Whence Victoria's self a Queen
   Rules the earth in glory.

White as snow the cliffs arise,
Black as night the soil impending.
Velvet green the pasture lies,
   Wave on wave extending.

O how rich this soil must be
Where the English oaks are planted,
Oaks which only to the free
   Have their garlands granted.

O how rich is he and blest
House and home who there has made him;
O how glorious there to rest
   Neath the oaks that shade him!

From "THE DREAM" [1]
(Transl. by G. M. Gathorne-Hardy.)

O'er the land there hung a haze
Like a veil, by fairy skill
Woven of the mirrored rays
From the heaven and from the brine;
Some were red and others blue,
It was thus the violet grew,
That behind the gauzes fine
Which the woods and meads distil
Draped the country's graceful line.
Darker in the misty weft
Every instant changed the hue;
Violet turned to dusky-grey,
And with closer meshes lay
The white lace above it spread:
But, when now and then 'twas cleft
By the evening breeze which drew
Towards us over Beachy Head,
Forward in the opening shot
Here and there a casual gleam
From the white cliff's frowning steep,

[1] Drømmesyn. From Den engelske Lods ("The English Pilot"), 1844.

As if giant ghosts should peep
From an open fairy grot,
Or a magic cauldron's steam
Forth in sudden disarray
Pallid as a moonbeam stray.

Through the night we only saw
Where the foam, all pearly white,
Sent a phosphorescent glow
Past the breaker's crest upraised,
Like the gleaming fangs which show
In a black sea-monster's maw:
    Farther still,
Sparkled either Foreland's light,
    Flames which blazed
Like the eyes of powers nocturnal,
Or a pair of fiends infernal,
Forced to watch the hours of night
By a mightier spirit's will.

Then—I own I cannot guess
How one single influence
Can enhance the spirit's sense
And the drowsy lids oppress;
But a spirit and a flower
Own, I deem, the self-same power:
    Midnight shades
Seal with sleep our human eyes,
While the soul, like bird in air,
Then most unrestrainéd flies,
So the blossom's glory fades,

But the scent
In its drooping calyx pent
Floats more poignant and more fair . . .
Then—the plash of waves around me
Lulled my heavy lids to close,
And the spell of night that bound me
Veiled my pupils in repose.
Over folded arms my brow
Rested on the gunwale now,
    But my sprite
Had to England ta'en its flight.

Rows of lights along the shore
(Lines of towns at evening traced,
Like a necklace closely strung
All along the Channel hung)
Woke my longing to explore,
Called my spirit there in haste.
Thither then at once it darted,
Swifter than the telegraphic
    Glance of love
Flashed 'twixt youth and maiden parted,
Gentler than the moon's seraphic
    Beams above
Tombs or windless waters glide;
As a silent moth at night
Through the sultry summer grove,
When on dust-grey wings it brushes
Under slumbering lilac-bushes,
All the joys such nights provide
Tasting to its heart's delight,—

Thus upon its course it started,
Wheresoe'er the fancy willed;
Through fair towns, their pomp and pride
Now in early slumber stilled,
Moving ever side by side
With the vessel on the tide.

All through Folkestone, Romney, Rye,
Hastings, ancient Winchelsea,
Did my spirit steer its way:
Where proud Brighton's streets are thrown
'Twixt her palaces of stone,
Like a single palace, cleft
In two rows to right and left:
And through woods, where in the dark
Many an eye sent forth a spark
(Poacher or majestic hart);
And through time-worn towns, where dwelt
Once the Saxon or the Celt,
Did my thought-borne spirit dart,
Dark on dark, unseen, unfelt,
Free and unrestrained, as though
'Twere my will that moved it so.

On each house a gable high
Nodded most familiarly
To its neighbour o'er the way,
As if each of these old chaps
Plotted how they might collapse
Both of them the self-same day:
Whispering how each was standing

Ere the Norman conqueror's landing,
Why not then like pals together
Reeling to the ground expire?
Wherefore wait for windy weather,
Or the chances of a fire?
Close at hand there stood the shell
Of a castle's battlement,
From whose loopholes' broken lines
Ivy-boughs as massive leant
As the coils a python twines.
In the high-street of the town
An old gate its solid pile
   Planted down,
Like a pigmy citadel,
Base from whence, with scrolls bedecked,
Lesser pinnacles project,
In a Saxo-Norman style.
Crownéd monarchs, carved in stone,
Grey with mould, their noses gone,
(On a limbless charger oft)
In their left hands held the triple
Curling lilies, while aloft
In their right a sword was borne;
   Smiles of scorn
Seemed across their lips to ripple
For the huckster race below,
Swarming in the ancient place,
Wielding canes for sword and bow,
While in place of helm a knitted
Cotton cap or wig was worn;
   Such a gear

To those shrunken brainpans fitted
As provoked a regal sneer
At the whole degenerate race.

Everywhere was silence deep
In those ancient towns, such blest
Solemn quiet that I heard
When some restless slumberer stirred,
Or a dreamer spoke in sleep;
Heard the strains a mother's tongue
  Softly sung,
As she lulled her babe to rest.

ENGLISH IVY [1]
(Transl. by G. M. Gathorne-Hardy.)

SOFTER, more harmonious lines
Finest brush with purest hue
  Never drew;
Nor the swelling wave designs,
Nor the fields of golden wheat,
Over which a zephyr chases:—
Than the green and wooded spaces
Where the Hampshire hills repeat
Each the other's sinuous way,
  By the Sound,
As its northward course is wound
Ever deeper up the bay.

[1] Engelsk Efeu. From Den engelske Lods ("The English
Pilot"), 1844.

Then I plainly understood
How my sires (I call them mine
Since from Sognefylke's sheer
Sea-encompassed savage crests,
Through those hardy warrior breasts,
Flowed the fervent strains of blood
To my own ancestral line)—
Then, ay then, I saw it clear,
How the viking, eagle-free,
And the Norman, who to France
Owed in part his chivalry,
In his conquering Duke's advance,—
How they both alike could share
In a passion strong as life
For thy form, with colour rife,
Lovely England, woman-fair!
   Yea, could come
To forget their native home,
Till their heart's roots they could sever
And abandon it for ever,
   To engraft
In an alien blood their own.
Where their conquering feet came down,
All around in ruins lay;
But, as in the Roman day,
Planted firm in earth the shaft
Of the victor's lance would stand,
So, where'er he chanced to land,
There the Norman raised a tower,
For an emblem of his power:
And those Norman castles stand

Still, symbolic, stout and grim,
Telling how that lovely land
All was once subdued by him.

But a yet more sovereign though
    Gentler foe
Has within those time-defaced
Walls the Norman conqueror based,
Entered with the force of right,
    As the site
Were his ancient heritage,
Which he would possess once more:
Fair as youth, though patriarch hoar
May not match his dateless age:
Born before the Saxon came,
He has watched each feudal claim
    Pass in sleep,
And from each abandoned keep
Long ago his banner flown:
Garland and triumphal crown
Over every arch has thrown,
Cornice, frieze and sill has decked
With the colours of his race,
Yea, and even the solid stone,
Torn at random from its place,
With his mighty arm has wrecked.
Mighty? Nay, how impotent
Seem those all-subduing arms,
As for childish pastime meant,
Though the while his pulses beat
With that vigorous blood that warms

Life with most enduring heat.
For that conqueror castle-storming,
Who the proudest race lives down,
Who, the dizzy ramparts swarming,
Trampling over noble dust,
Leaves his fluttering pennons set
On each crumbling parapet,—
He none other is but just
Immemorial England's own
   Heir avowed,
Her symbolic ivy green,
Fair, with changeless youth endowed,
Growing wildly o'er the scene;
Cherished lover of the proud
English oak-tree's loyal breed,
Verdant Nature's Ganymede.

Say that Portsmouth were to close
All her crowded barrack rows,
Let the "Queen" and all the fleet,
One by one, in tale complete,
High and dry on shore be set,—
Rotting ribs and seams that yawn—
On the beach, as whales are drawn,
Gasping, floundering in a net:
Then, before three years were flown,
Fleet and town and citadel,
Forts and barrack rows as well,
All would then be overgrown
By an ivy jungle, vanished
Wholly, as the stars are banished,

When a cloud obscures the view,
As you search for them anew.
In and out by every gate,
Every shattered window pane,
Over ruins desolate,
From the upper storeys falling,
Like a mighty serpent crawling,
Would the wanton ivy creep:
Round the wreck's bare ribs would strain,
In and out of every swart
Deadly grinning battle-port
Sturdy branch and leaf would sweep:
As with anchor chains confined,
All those bows together bind,
Weave together, cable-fast,
Spar to spar and mast to mast,
  Rig them all
With its tendrils tough and tall,
As with seaman's hands, at last.

Yea, if London now lay dead,—
Should her crowds no more engage
In the ceaseless strife they wage
With the green of Nature's land,
As their walls for aye expand,
Deeper in the country thrown:—
If by every road they fled,
Swarming out, as worms retreat
When they've nothing left to eat,
From that town-absorbing town;
Leaving it as waste as is

Eden's old metropolis,
Dead as stately Babylon,
Niniveh and Ctesiphon:—
Long ere many years were flown,
England's ivy host would then
Turn victorious back again,
Tear the pavement stone from stone,
Over London Bridge would strain,
  Tightly knot
Lordly hall to labourer's cot,
Round St. Paul's its garlands bind,
In a net of leaves entwined
  Make the Tower
Like a hive or sylvan bower;
Bond Street would at length be made
Like a covered close arcade,
Changed be every formal square
To a theatre green and rare,
All with living scenery filled,
Where, to music softly trilled,
Finch and linnet might approve—
In a sweet love-comedy—
Histrionic talents high,
Though above,
In a critical array,
Captious starlings damned the play.

London would become a lonely
Wood, where e'en St. Pauls was swallowed,
One vast wilderness, that followed
Lovely Nature's order only.

There would dwell in Paradise
Countless birds and butterflies,
And from cloudless skies once more,
On a London purged at last
From the foulness of her past,
Pure and pardoning sunlight pour.

TO NIELS DAHL [1]
(Transl. by J. Bithell.)

Give me a flask of Health's wine,
　　And take my fame away!
Though melancholy you will be,
　　I shall be glad and gay.

Send me a leaf of Hope's tree,
　　And take my laurel crown!
When you are tired of it, before
　　Your donkey cast it down!

Give me the feelings of your heart,
　　And you take mine instead!
Accounts will balance then, I think,—
　　Judging by what you've said!

The thistle by the dusty road
　　Is not so thorned as fame.
O that I owned two acres of ground,
　　And Peter were my name!

[1] Pastor Niels Dahl, a member of the Storthing, had written
a greeting in verse to Wergeland in "Morgenbladet".

146

A plot of earth myself should till!
  It is of Heaven to dream!
A straw hat, and a grey smock,
  A cottage by the stream!

But I will live and I will die
  With tender harp that thrills.
Most precious thing on earth it is,
  And comforts all my ills.

Famous? Ah well! Tobacca and pipe,
  If health again should find me . . .
Only give me 'bacca and pipe,
  And I will thank you kindly.

I ask no fame save that which you,
  And a few besides, admit—
For the Shah's and Czar's and Sultan's wealth
  I would not barter it.

ON THE SICK-BED [1]
(Transl. by G. M. Gathorne-Hardy.)

THESE stabs of flame, this icy thrill
Which shivers through my breast—
Call them thy triumph, Death, they bring
To me the wayward airs of spring
Stirring in Heaven, now warm, now chill,
The April of my rest.

But still my heart, in steadfast fight,
Invading Death defies;

[1] Paa Sygeleiet. 1844.

Still stoutly beating, day by day,
Undaunted keeps the foe at bay:
My spirit, tranquil, clear and bright,
Like moonlit water lies.

So then, perchance, I yet may know
My briar[1] in all its bloom,
Whose springing shoots at first were seven,
Then grew to nine, and now eleven,
And others yet, I trust, may grow,
Should Death delay his doom.

Ah! flower as where in Gulistan
The Persian roses stand!
Yet none your hidden plot will seek,
Ye blossom in the desert bleak,
Where I was driven, a banished man,
From kindred and from land.

Yes, to this barren loneliness
Driven by my country's ban,
By raging fools, who little guess
How glorious here the woods are grown,
Where I have lived, like cage-bird flown,
Or ranging Indian.

Brazil's inviolate forest, where
The lofty palm tree towers,
Whose stem the gay camellias twine,
Blent with the blue of passion-flowers,

[1] The work on which the poet was engaged, Jødinden, "The Jewess, eleven blossoming briar shoots", and to which this poem was prefaced.

Has naught to show so proud, so fair
As this lone haunt of mine.

Here too of visions is no lack,
Here spirit forms intrude;
Like clouds that ever onward creep
Through woodland boughs in lowering wrack,
Grey memories oft would past me sweep,
Here in the solitude.

Yet must I, in my loved retreat,
Some deadly hurt have ta'en
From sorcery or serpent's bite,—
My arm is weak, my cheek is white,
My pulses now so feebly beat,
Dark is my every vein.

Ah! mighty Death's compelling blast
My thread of life has torn;
I fain would drag me to my kind,
I long to tell them where to find
This garden which I planted last,
Flowering in wastes forlorn.

Lo! Drips there not a honeyed sap
From every budding rose?
Does not each open petal bear
A song of love enscrolléd there?
Does not each blossom's purple lap
A sacred book disclose?

Could I but respite win from Death
Till every bloom were grown!
But all about I feel his breath,

He chokes me in his bony gripe,
And from his fell and stealthy pipe
The noiseless dart has blown.

Ah, sense of cleansing, pure, intense;
I have forgiven all!
A finger lightly touched my brow,—
An angel's, 'twas my mother's call:
A dew-washed flower my soul is now,
New-born in innocence.

A VOICE IN THE WILDERNESS [1]
(Transl. by G. M. Gathorne-Hardy.)

HEARTS of Christians all should glow
With the warmth of Christmas fare,
   Honey-sweet,
Heaped for all the world to eat,
Should it chance to enter there;
Decked with sprigs of roses gay,
As for festal holiday.
   Woe! Woe!
Ice they are, or lumps of snow,
Stones, within whose crannies dwell
Swarms obscene from blackest hell;
All their softness merely mould,
Though like velvet to behold.

And a clear, transparent sheen
Should on every brow be seen,
Like that radiance milky-white

---

[1] Røst i Ørkenen. From Jødinden ("The Jewess"), 1844.

Where a star would pierce the night:
Gentle smiles on every face,
Eloquent, with kindness blest,
As if all the human race
Were its loved and welcome guest.
    Woe! Woe!
Reckoning tablets dark and drear
Hide those noble aspects now,
    To and fro
Ciphered o'er twixt either brow;
And with tears of maudlin passion,
And of vice the maniac leer,
—Features all in savage fashion
    Bruised and scarred—
Is the nation's visage marred.

Quenched the fire of love departs,
As the colour from the rose,
And the people shut their hearts
Like a miser's coffer close;
While a cold estranging mind
Severs each man from his kind,
As when some poor wanderer tramps
Through the city streets alone,
Where in every pane the lamps
Are extinguished one by one.
"Give me shelter!" he will plead;
    Who will heed?
Shake, for 'tis the wisest plan,
From thy feet the dust, O man!
Shun this town, and seek the lee

Of some friendlier forest tree:
Turks and savages possess
More fraternal kindliness
And humanity than we.

As with him who wandered lonely
Through the waste, deserted town,
Haunted by the echoes only
From the trodden pavement thrown,
Such the poet's hapless lot
Who receives in trust from heaven
Oil for empty vessels given,
And that charge betrayeth not,
Trifling for the world's delight;
But still strikes in lyric chords
Harmonies to God's own words,
Sounds the solemn call of right,
Where o'er duties long foregone
Errant hearts are barred with stone.
   Woe! Woe!
Once we all of us have sworn
Troth beneath God's roof, and worn
Crowns of innocence that day,
Crowns which in a year decay;
Women round their heads have wreathed
Garlands fresh of roses white,
Where the purple scarce has breathed;
Men, that day, in open sight—
Though perchance with less display—
Wore at least a little spray.
But the promise which they gave,

Full persuaded,
And in accents clear and deep,
    Was to keep
And to carry to the grave,
Hearts untainted and unfaded
As those flowers the day they trod
In the presence of their God.

O 'twas then, with sinless sight,
God ye saw, and how he spanned
Utmost depth and farthest height;
How the fly of nameless race
In the same encircling hand
Fluttered, turned itself or crept
As the proudest stars that swept
'Tween the viewless arms of space:
And ye felt ye too might nurse
In your arms the universe,
Earth and heavenly spheres combined,
That no lesser bliss ye knew
While ye to your bosoms drew
As your brethren all mankind.

THE MAPLE AND THE PINE [1]
(Transl. by G. M. Gathorne-Hardy.)

The Pine.

WHAT makes such pleasant strains at eve
    Among thy branches high?
Which e'en my gloomy boughs awake
    Almost to gaiety.

[1] Jeg er nu saadan Jeg. From Jødinden ("The Jewess"), 1844.

The Maple.
It is a merry swarm of bees,
Allowed a shelter here;
Since when the forest hardly holds
A tree of blither cheer.

Music I have the whole day long
Exchanged for nothing more
Than leave to sip some honey from
My crown's abundant store.

Each twig is full of active life,
My smallest leaves supply
(Where lazy grubs were wont to crawl)
The food of industry.

Honey and wax are stored within
The yaffle's empty nest;
A heart that's full of tender love
Seems hidden in my breast.

The Pine.
Aha! So foreigners you let
Suck out your sweetness all?
Rather would I before the storm
My dear spring shoots should fall.

And all my golden pollen I
Would scatter to the breeze,
Ere I would suffer in my shade
Such alien guests as these.

Like molten silver on the rock
My turpentine I pour,
As I have done a hundred years,
And shall for evermore.

The Maple.
Admit the bee, a cake of wax
Shall well requite the deed.

The Pine.
Honey and wax? A century
I've lived, nor felt their need.

I represent my native land;
That task is all I care
To live for, and for others I
Have therefore naught to spare.

The Maple.
Drive then away all active life,
And joy of life as well,
And be a century more the place
Where none but beggars dwell.

The dish love proffers free to all,
Without parade or show,
Ne'er lacks the meed of recompense
Which grateful guests bestow.

Give sap, and honey takes its place,
Shelter, and songs will sound,
Give liberty, dark pine, and get
The life you see I found.

Hark what a merry bustle stirs
In that old linden tree:
He has a hospitable mind—
Just that, no more—like me.

His spreading top, as in my case,
With swarms of bees is crowned;
Each branch is now a factory thronged,
Where wealth is piled around.

The willow and the rowan too!
Look round, thou canny pine!
For all about examples teach
A happier way than thine.

The Pine.

Humph! Has not idleness a smack
Of sweetness? Is't not so?
And has not solitude its charms?
I'm built that way, you know.

FOLLOW THE CALL![1]
(Transl. by G. M. Gathorne-Hardy.)

ROYAL eagle, captive made,
Broken-winged, with fettered limb,
He that twenty years and more—
Since the shot that crippled him—
Plies the humble watch-dog's trade
By a lonely cottage door,
Cannot know

[1] Følg Kaldet! From Jødinden ("The Jewess"), 1844.

All the wretched poet's woe,
Of a little nation born,
In a spot remote, forlorn,
With a speech
Which can never further reach
Than the uttered breath may go.

He is like a bell, men hush,
Muffled close in clammy folds;
Like the rose's radiant bush
Which a covering basket holds;
For to give his genius wing,
Or his spirit's bounds to spurn,
Like his happier mates who sing
Where the millions listening stand,
Were to will the world to turn
In a cask's confining band.

Rather be an Indian,
Native-born, a savage child,
Midst the tribes in tropics wild,
Or an Araucanian.
These will hail the bard as priest,
Carry him to every feast,
Build for him a leafy bower,
Sit and listen, hour by hour,
By his fire, and learn his song
Strain by strain,
And in chorus his refrain
Carol jubilant and strong.
Last, the old, when he shall die,

Gather all his minstrelsy,
While the young
Learn it from an elder's tongue.

Other light than what at times
Flashes from the poet's lays
Ne'er these humble ones descry;
Virtues, crimes,
Wandering by their several ways
Home to immortality,
For the final judge to try—
'Twas the bard who guessed them first,
To his tribe in songs rehearsed;
Yea, the thought
Of the Spirit they revere
Folk benighted owe the seer
Who alone the vision caught.
Like to gems which cast a sheen
Through the waves that roll between,
Through the gloom of savage lays
Wondrous revelations blaze.

Ah, but we ourselves are still
Savages in mind and will,
Yea, and often in our actions:
Not the Indians of the West
By such rancour are possessed,
Though their thirst with blood they sate,
Tribes that forests separate,
As our Europe, rent in factions
By the bitterest party hate.

Young as yet the world must be;
All our long, long history
Still is but its cradle-song,
And its childhood's fairy-tale.
Creatures of the prime prevail:
Megasaurs in forests sleep,
Jonah's monster haunts the deep,
Giant serpents, vast and strong,
Wastes, a thousand miles along,
Thousands o'er,
Thundering with the lion's roar,
Mock our busy human ways:
Mountains, as in Noah's days,
Undecayed,
Still their splintered peaks parade;
Not a sign is yet revealed
That to earth at last that shoulder
Down shall moulder,
To create a fruitful field.
Nay, but mark yon mountain rude,
Glittering like a crystal clear,
Where the precipice falls sheer,
Heavenly blue or violet-hued:
What that Alpine horn has ploughed,
Smoothed its flank and polished bright,
Piece by piece and grain by grain?
Drops of rain:
Just the gentle touch of white
Atom-woven cloaks of cloud,
Plumes upon the helm of mist.
What has ground the rock to sand,

Washed away the ruddy schist,
Till the heaps beneath expand,
Purer, whiter, at the base?
Falling water, soft and round,
Yonder ocean's measured pace,
Lapping billows, blithely curled,
Ever in a stir profound,
Like the breathing of a world;
While in summer-time the moss,
Through millenniums long to tell,
Tiny silver cups will toss
On the crag's grey barren shell,
Till in scattered bloom at last
Lofty pines are rooted fast.

There is nothing, great or small,
Nothing fruitless, no decay,
There is purpose in its fall,
Howso vaguely cast away;
Fallen dews,
Steaming up in sunny heat,
In the cloud's wide bosom meet,
Like a veil that flutters gay,
Woven but of blossom-hues;
And the slender downy flakes
Spun by ancient willow-trees,
Busy as the wife who makes
Wraps against a winter day,
Drift not lost adown the breeze;
For the ant, where'er they come,
Draws them thence to make his home.

Must the poet's word, the pure
Dew of light's own sparks, that start
Warm as blood from out his heart,
Here, where all things else endure,
Unremembered and untraced,
Disappear and run to waste?
Up! If God's own voice invest
With a storm thy heaving breast:
Cry aloud in desert ways,
And the dawn of better days
From the dark thy word shall raise.
Up! If hands that sweep the string
To the sound of noble lays
Radiant light in darkness fling.
From that little rugged crowd,
Inarticulate and cowed,
Some shall yet—like Lapps who dwell
On a wild and stony fell,
Called by sight of flames afar
From the hovel where they are—
Hasten where the bard afire
Tunes the sinews of his lyre,—
And, when next he lifts his gaze,
There his scanty audience stays,
Serves his ends,
He will crave no longer now
Thronging millions ranged below,
Just a little band of friends.

From "WANTON WEEDS" [1]
(Transl. by G. M. Gathorne-Hardy.)

It is quite unjust to state—
As so often it is said—
The poetic age is dead
Since . . . But who can fix the date?
Would you have my private view,—
Times so unromantic grew
Just when he who grumbles thus
Had to flog his Pegasus,
Who was sleepy, lazy, lean,
Just as if his mount had been
On a miserable screw:
When, like stream in sand that ceases,
Petered out the poet's vein;
When his pen was gnawed to pieces,
And the blood boiled in his brain:
Off in smoke his fancies flew,
And the nightingale conceded
Cuckoos sang as well as he did.

'Tis a lie, a shame, a slight
Done to Nature's fresh delight,
Ever bursting forth anew,
Or the sun, which scales the heaven
Every day as clear and bright
As on that first morn when through
Parted clouds his beams were driven.
Did the dew that on that day
Woke the flowers on Eden's lawn

[1] Kaadt Ukrudt. From Jødinden ("The Jewess"), 1844.

Sparkle with a purer ray
Than returns each summer dawn?
Are not all these stars the same—
Which above our faces flame—
As Euphrates' shepherds knew
In those quiet nights which shone
On the plains of Babylon,
Whence their mystic lore they drew?
Waste indeed is Eden's bower,
But assuredly unchanged
Over all the earth have ranged
Pink and rose and passion-flower.
Stocks and dahlias grace each plot,
Baby-eyed forget-me-not,
Wallflowers, tulips gaily dressed,
Oleanders and the rest
Of that loveliness, than which
Even a poet's fantasy,
By his death made doubly free,
Can imagine naught more splendid,
With an art sublimer blended,
Dowered with form more fair and rich.
O we should in Nature strive,
Then, to let our spirits live,
Mid these wonders manifold,
Sights from Paradise transplanted,
Which while centuries have rolled
In unchanging grace survive
By an added mercy granted.
Nature knows not of decay,
Naught of years or ages knows

In her blest eternal day
Which, begun, shall never close.

Though we dress no longer in
Rude Arcadian coats of skin,
As in those fair ages gone
When through Hellas Orpheus played,
Followed close by stock and stone;
At whose tuneful coming must
    Hermes' bust
Limbless dance adown the glade;
Yet, while most in sleep are laid,
Still such miracles are wrought
That we think (a happy thought
'Tis to some, to others pain)
That in wide creation's chain
Girding us on every side,
In the tree that arches wide
By the door, and every year
In the flowers that reappear,
We have watchers of our fate
Wiser, more articulate,
Than the world imagines here.

TO AN ILLUSTRIOUS POET [1]
(Transl. by I. Grøndahl.)

By Mjøsen, the heart of my country loud-beating
                                    beneath
The full breasts of Heidmark, where Helgey arises,

[1] Henrik Steffens, to whom—with six other "spokesmen of truth" the first edition of Wergeland's *magnum opus*, "Creation," was dedicated, in 1830.

Blushing pride of the motherly bosom . . .
Where Skreya, midsummer-sun's hostel with golden-
                red open
Cloud-gate, where the storm's whinnying foal and the
                vapours'
Car rest thro' the night, at morning to foam o'er the
                waters . . .
Where headlong into the waves the mount plunges,
A birch rises up, with anxious rustle and dizzily bent
            at once springing back . . .

There a boy with his harp is sitting . . . Hear, ten of
            its strings
Sound like the slow bells of sadness, like notes of the
            blackbird—
Ten like fire-spluttering Hell do shriek, thrice ten
Hymn-trembling temple resounding.   [like a

Fifty harp-strings? Nay, golden kingdoms of Stella!

But hush! Lonely they sigh like the valley
No wanderer visits.

And over them all now sorrow is ruling,
An old jaundiced monk.

Fifty harp-strings? Ay, golden kingdoms of Stella!

The throne is deserted, and they
'Neath an ocean of anarchy moaning.

Then, Stella, like free Tomyris,
Reign over howling desert!

Waste where no echo would answer
Even thy name, shouldst thou cry.

Alas! or live in thy oasis,
Lone like Zenobia proud!

Thy eyes—lo! living sources!
Thy lips—roses of Jericho!

Thy cheek is a palm-grove
In sunrise glowing!

Thy teeth—Palmyrean columns,
Built of alabaster!

But, woe! Legions are coming,
Days frosty are coming.

Thy bosom 'neath the yoke darkening,
Thy heart droops like a conquered banner.

The pillars of Tadmor are broken.
Moths flutter by . . . Now stillness is reigning.

Then, where is then Stella? Lo, here is my harp
With one broken string!

Not till in Heaven, tho' hardly a bow-shot from
Skreya,
A leap from my seat 'neath the trembling bent birch,
Shall I recover the broken one whole;
Stella kneeling entwines it.

'It broke,' she will say; 'that time thou with anxious
Calling my feigned playful flight didst pursue.

We were running—rash play!—in a church-yard,
We both stumbled into a grave.'

'Hush, loved one, hush!'—thus I interrupt her—
'I found thee at last in thy flight:
Did I not seize thee 'mongst stars?
Immortality is our dowry;
Beams our wedding-garment,
Thine white as the stars, mine silvery golden;
On the heights of the blest stands our home;
Messiah weds us for Eternity;
The seraphs strike up; we dance thro' radiant Heaven.'

Now—Bard!—my sadness is joy, my joy becomes
      song 'neath the birch tree,
Song, song between Heaven and Earth, up here where
      a pair of
Eagles that nigh have hidden their nest, swift-rushing
      do fan me,
Song, song of Heaven and Earth, song of the nature
      of Souls.
For see! Like the falcon to loftiest solitude rising—
Just when the ring-dove it missed, then soaring most
      calmly,
E'en tho' as nothing had happened—I seek consolation
Here in my castle of solitude 'gainst the maid's
      hardness:

Here on my mount, on my dizzy ledge with the birch-
tree,
Here on my mound, my soft flowering hillock where
every
Sorrow at once is turned into heavenly visions.
There now is leaning my head while pondering deep
the
Nature of Love, on how it can be that a woman—
Coy as the white water-lily so fair that floats 'neath
the surface,
Altho' its corolla is ripe and full like the young
maiden's bosom—
Power has my soul to govern, my strong will, alone,
without limit,
As if in each look a blue-glimmering steel net were
thrown—
Power has the beat of my heart absolutely to measure:
Soon as the bell 'gainst the temple-wall, or as the
billows
Break on the rocks; then again—by a casual smile—
Slow with inaudible beat, softly as butterfly-wings.

Ah! Three seconds peace, and my soul's at the
Realms of thought and of dreaming.   [borders of
Spirits already accost me,
Some of them speaking, others just beckoning mild.

'Hush!'—one is whisp'ring—'Once in the days of
Pair of seraphs did seek them   [creation a
Homes in Adam's and Eve's
Slumbering hearts; from them you both do descend.

Alas! They could not recognise one another—but
Secretly feel one another.   [vaguely,
This feeling the love of
Man and of woman, mighty tho' groping and blind.

One spirit himself from Heaven did banish; the other
Self-sacrificing did follow.
Self-sacrifice is heavenly
Love's inmost law, spirit to spirit in Love.'

. . . How like 'tis the Love of the Saviour!
O dear, tender, tender Mother!
I will sing of Heaven's Love only,
My own love, the earthly, forgetting.

What foolish prattle! This love is
Descended also from Heaven!
Our heavenly names now I know,
Wherewith in our graves we are christened.

The spirit I have seen that lived in
Adam's heart—me he resembled—
And that which to Eve's heart its life gave . . .
I recognised thee in the blest one!   [O Stella!

Like the spirit thou too once shalt wear
A wreath of Heaven's starry blossoms,
Thy heritage costly; then shall I step forth
From clouds where far off I was kneeling.
With shining flowers from the garland then
Shalt thou strew my head full proudly,
Whose promise bold I redeem when I sing
The Marriage of Heaven and Earth.

Oh! daring design! . . . I tremble.
All Nature has heard it.
Rustling the birch to the lake gave it,
Rushing the lake to the shore rolls it.
Thund'ring the All breaks upon me:
'See, Poet! Am I not Love, Love alone?
Forget not the stars! Forget not the flower!
Forget not the worm in the dust!'

And the stars, one by one, are approaching,
Like full, shining sails;
Beasts break out from the forest,
Hemming me in with kind looks;
Rises the snake in the heather,
Proud as a king who his kingdom is viewing;
The flowers, their hearts to disclose, are
Opening all.
All wants to be sung in the Love-poem,
All that is having come out of Love.

Anguish! anguish! I am o'erwhelmed
By heavenly visions and greatness of worlds,
By the motley whirl of the living.
Myriad-voiced the All rushes on me,
Confuses with thick-crowding visions—
That I, who should in the midst of its zenith
Sit like immovable eye, solitary,
Am whirl'd on myself, like a mote among motes.

Illustrious Poet! Would by my harp thou wert seated,
Thy hands to my brow sweet coolness returning:
The laurels for which it is burning!

THE TWO SPIRITS [1]

(Transl. by G. M. Gathorne-Hardy.)

Phun-Abiriel [2] *and Ohebiel* [3] *over the steaming empty world.*

Phun-Abiriel.

SEE, from the teeming womb of Space again
A new world born: a last new mystery.

Ohebiel.

Kneel and adore in God's fresh smoking tracks.

Phun-Abiriel.

Is God, then, in this lump? Shall this be worshipped?

Ohebiel.

He this dank slime has quickened. See, it breathes.

Phun-Abiriel.

Ay, bow, ye spirits, to a lifeless God,
Since nameless and invisible the true;
To this, corruption's bare triumphal arch,
Raised for Death's festival, which soon begins,
With the first grass that rises from the mire,
Life's flowering banner . . .
With the proud army of creation
As ranks of victims midmost in the train
Which ends with gliding pomp of victor worms.
Yea, bow, ye spirits; yonder in the dust
An image was our God; here 'tis a globe.
Symbol and faith—for certainty is hid

---

[1] Opening Scene of Mennesket ("Man"). Revised Edition
of Skabelsen ("Creation"), 1845.
[2] A vigorous sceptical spirit.
[3] A loving spirit.

Like life-drops in the Eternal's inmost heart—
Are still the milk for babes which feeds your wisdom.
Ay, bow, ye spirits, to that lump of earth!
Since all your wisdom, which inspired would fly
On dawn-red wings of immortality
Through all the barren upland wastes of Space—
Till God ye saw, until His sea of light
Flowed at your feet,—behold, it stops and sinks
In this morass! From prophet-heights inspired
Your soul will by this lump be dragged down, down
To depths of madness, if it thinks thereon;
And all its happiness will be dissolved,
As clouds in dew, by this same lifeless steam,
Which spurs so vainly its intelligence.
Yet will I ponder, though it wear me out.

Ohebiel.

O Phuniel, thou my sorrow, filled with doubts!
Abiriel, the courageous, my delight!
O Phun-Abiriel, whom I love and mourn,
Where else but brooding over steaming spheres,
In wait for God, yea, e'en in life's conception,
Shall I, distracted, find Abiriel?

Phun-Abiriel.

Where is that God? 'Tis but His might I see,
Hear but the hum of worlds his feet have stirred
Like clouds of dust: I gaze, but see no more,
Ah! naught but the deep eddy of his track,
Wherein to madness, though it may not drown,
My soul is whirled. Ha! were my fancy not

So light and void, dark as this globe 'twould roll
Visibly forth, and I, like God, create.
For though a spirit, and albeit I am
Straight borne to wheresoe'er my fancy flies,
Yet when I think on God, and look for Him,
Then stand I where I stood when spoke the thought,
Stunned by the noise of all His roaring worlds.

Ohebiel.

Yet shall my tender love, unhappy spirit,
Thy pondering for ever clear and guide,
Like the brave torch which presses through the dark,
Piercing with shafts of flame the heart of midnight:
And I will speak, to cheer its loneliness,
And gently answer its wild questionings.

Phun-Abiriel.

Ohebiel, thou seest a shade that clouds
Through all my form and substance starry clear,
Outspreading from my inmost consciousness;
These are my tears, and this Abiriel's thanks.

Ohebiel.

Bethink thee, then, how impious, that a spirit
But newly loosed from dust—for heaven has since
Turned but a thousand times—should yet demand
To see the Eternal. Haply such an end
The oldest spirits might reach, who, like Akadiel,
Have lived a life on long extinguished stars.
Think, if thou knewest how grows a blade of grass,

Creation's key thou heldest in thy hand;
But lo! While but the steam of scarce-born spheres
Is all thy pondering's morbid sustenance,
Its dew, whereby it waxes in its gloom,
And all the worlds riddle on riddle piled,—
Lo! Phuniel, all the other spirits blest,
Yea, e'en Akadiel, first-born of them all,
O'er every new-created world rejoice,
As 'twere a flower on the Creator's track,
Sprung on His journey through the Universe:
For well they know 'tis framed for happiness.
And, Phun-Abiriel, remember too
That thou wast conjured by the gentle sun
Of the Almighty and All-Merciful,
A spirit, from dust, a spirit, to endure
Though all the worlds like blossoms fade and die;
And that almighty perfect wisdom was
The gentle current—though of giant force—
Which tore thee on like the blind seed, which yonder
Grows to a shoot and after to a palm.

Phun-Abiriel.

I have but recollection, and on this
Am nourished, like a beast that chews the cud.

Ohebiel.

Of spirits' knowledge is not that the heart?
As round the heart the body, all their wisdom
Grows round the memories of their first existence.
The first word, treasured in a mother's ear,
The spirit still retains, as freshly writ,

And thou with thy first conscious thought hast
And sucked the breast of immortality.   [grasped
But, Phuniel, as we contemplate the world,
Knowledge, the sustenance of deathless souls,
Is given the spirit in measureless profusion,
And with his knowledge still his power will grow.
Like twins, who to their fond embraces seem
Their growth and similarity to owe,
So wax they in each other's fire and light,
Till all eternity's too strait, and falls
As childhood's garments from the youth full-grown.
And still the heap of life's experience
Grows ever for the spirit; 'tis his mount
Whereon he builds his wisdom's citadel,
Whence he surveys afar the Universe.

Phun-Abiriel.

Yet what a distance from the infinite!
What comes of all this staring into Space—
Sphere of God's thought—but veneration dumb?
Such veneration crushes, not uplifts.

Ohebiel.

O, 'tis the spirit's love and sacrifice
To Him, the Eternal.

Phun-Abiriel.

        'Tis a sluggard's couch,
Wherein all energy is lulled to sleep.
But from this couch has Phuniel arisen,
And probes with wakened eyes eternity.

Ohebiel.
Probe not for God. Be happy as a child,
Who still mid spirits art a child indeed.
Disport thine eye with beauty of His worlds,
Hope all things of thine immortality,
Who sawest, though youthful yet, worlds pass away.

Phun-Abiriel.
Am I among the spirits but a child?
Was not that globe which now so redly flames
My cradle, where I woke to consciousness
Mid animals and plants most wonderful?
That was my childhood's playground, where I grew
Till I discarded, as the snake his skin,
The lovely robe of sense which wrapped me round,
And like a snake, bare as a thunderbolt,
Came from the soil into the waste of Space:
'Twas then my childhood ended.

Ohebiel.
Copy then
Youth's confidence, my Phuniel!

Phun-Abiriel.
Ay, but wherefore
Can I not see my Father?

Ohebiel.
Dost not see
Skirts of His raiment hanging o'er the deep?
The billowing of their dark folds in its steam?

And in yon starry arch His girdle's gems?
When thou hast read His poem, the Universe,
And learnt the hymn of praise of perfect love,
Then hope and trust that thou shalt see His face.

Phun-Abiriel.

On hope's frail reed must spirits also lean?
And shall faith's rainbow-coloured shade, which we
Bore, as the Kings of dust, above our heads,
And swore deceitfully was Heaven itself—
Fearing our reason else would fly astray
When over her she saw the free, the true,
While ties of flesh and blood still fettered her
To earth—shall this o'er-tent the spirits still?
Nay, Phuniel's faith shall be but what he knows.
To grasp and to believe with us is one.
God wills not we unworthily should trust
What He has not permitted us to grasp—
Granting our souls sufficient strength for that.
That which I comprehend I first believe,
And add it to my lore as treasure trove.

Ohebiel.

Then is the kernel of thy knowledge faith;
Thy faculties but fight faith's battle.

Phun-Abiriel.
Yes,
Till no enigma, neither that which now
The dewdrop hides—the key to all existence—
Nor the "God"-puzzle ravelled round myself
Shall still remain unsolved.

Ohebiel.

Eternity
Is the wide field, where victory shall be won.

Phun-Abiriel.
I reel then, weary at the spectacle
Where the eternal in the eternal glides,
Like to a ring without or joint or end.

Ohebiel.
Couldst find a joint, the ring were wrought amiss,
Thou tear, that restless glidest round the ring!
But see Akadiel's triumphant joy,
As though the summit of his aims were reached,
Whence he could see the Everlasting, past
The distance which no creature oversteps,
And mirrored His reflexion in his face.
Of spirits he is first. Yet he admires
With deepest ecstasy, his goodness reaches
Farthest, most childlike is his joy in all;
So that a flower he has not seen before,
Fair past conception, oft, on distant worlds,
Spurs him to songs of praise. Lo! Phuniel,
Thus the first spirit enjoys his blessed state,
And so canst thou.

Phun-Abiriel.
If he and I were one,
And not as different as earth and sky.

Ohebiel.
Him do the spirits strive to imitate,
For then they feel that they are likest God.

Phun-Abiriel.

If I believed it, I would slay my freedom,
Wash throughly from my soul the thought of God,
And grave Akadiel's image only there—
A spirit like myself—and charge myself
With guilt, each time I thought not as he thinks.

Ohebiel.

O Phuniel, know thou yet, that is forbidden,
Yea, by that right, wherein all share alike,
Ennobling dust to Godhead, that of striving
Far down the path which each one's freedom clears
With independent strength as each deems best,
To copy that whence he and all have sprung.
It is the children's right, that every child
Portrays his father's virtue and his strength
In his own nature's colours. We are all
Children of God, down from the first-born, who
In farthest ages lay in swaddling bands,
But now and ever takes precedence o'er
His kin, because he clearest wears of all
His father's lineaments in his ripe beauty,
To youngest, who, by sensuous fragrance lulled,
Unconscious in the grass Life's bosom sucks,
Still without form or mind, and hardly more
Than a warmed clod, unlike his origin,
More than the hour-old embryo his father.
And 'tis the spirit's heritage, that each
To the divinity from which he sprang
Shall make his own approach, by self-made way,
Winged independent through eternity.

Thence, Phuniel, comes that confidence in self
Which in quick touches on the inner soul,
On the broad marble surface of its calm,
Can paint the bliss, which is the work of art
Peculiar to each fancy and each heart.

Phun-Abiriel.

Such art, methinks, would madness best achieve;
It has imagination, hues of flame,
And madness and all-wisdom are the only
Things which the tooth of doubt may never gnaw.
If then I could—were't not a dragon chained
Fast in the dust—I would set madness free:
For as it bore me on, with smiles for wings,
To every goal I fancied, it would reach me—
With a triumphant laughter plucked apart—
Each riddle that I pointed at, and when
It angled, with a crooked guess for hook,
In the great deep, straight, as the line was cast,
'Twould fish me up the pearl of my desire.
My madness on elastic limbs would leap
Over each bar, where wisdom, deep beneath,
Must grope her way by countless reasonings,
Sane but how slow, to find an entrance way.
Thus, O Ohebiel, were I mad enough
To think, "I am God," then I should feel the bliss
That's proper to a God.

Ohebiel.

Be it enough that all around is good,
That, even to superfluity, the good

Is fair in hue and form, that, out of sight,
God's greatness grows. In this we have a share,
As heirs by birth, so far as we can grasp it.
His perfect goodness hast thou in such measure
As from thy goodness for thyself thou metest,
And in His perfect wisdom sharest, if
Thyself art wise . . .
Glow with a spirit's joy, then, shining through
The semblance which God's tender fantasy
Gave us, that as our strength and virtue bloom,
And as our kinder instincts issue forth,
Its morning sheen should blossom yet more fair,
And all our substance be a robe of beauty.
Here does no form speak false, as in that sphere
Where vice was sparkling and where virtue dulled;
The spirit good and wise has beauty too.
But O, thy gloom, that spirit's canker, since
Thou canst not solve the riddle of thyself—
Whose parts are scattered in infinity,
A chain of links stretched from the earliest sun
Down to the insect's wing—makes pale thy beauty,
Which should be a reflexion of thy joy.
Phuniel, my grief, Abiriel, my pride,
Two powers within thee strive for mastery;
O let that triumph which believes that Nature
Is God's majestic temple, and this earth
A new-raised column, immortality
The dawn-dyed cupola, o'erarching all
Spirits, who like a perfect hymn of praise
Pour through the portals of eternity.
Then glow thou in the spirits' common joy,

In their conviction of their blessedness;
For God, we know, is near, our goodness now
A greater part of God's perfection,
Our power and insight in the Universe
A share of perfect wisdom, perfect power,
Greater than when, drunk with the blood of life,
We, shadowed by the looming wings of Death,
Would sit together, joined by mutual love,
Upon a lower step of God's high throne,
And found our joy in lording over thousands
Of animals and plants.

Phun-Abiriel.

Soon shall these clouds have fought their latest fight;
The sunbeam pierces onward to this earth.
Then will it move no longer as asleep,
Nor rock as gently as a cradle, but
Its flight begins: intoxicate with light,
As it had drained the beaker of the sun,
With rainbow harp, and wreath of morning cloud,
Shall it begin its frolic through the void.
The happy beasts are this world's shout of joy,
And flowers and trees its wilding fantasy.
Then, whilst all other spirits throng together
To view this drama which is ever new,
Then do I turn away; for then well forth
The clouded sources of my discontent;
For I, who penetrate through flesh and bone
To read the thoughts of souls on all these spheres,
Reel dazzled from these miracles of light,
Nor comprehend its painting in the flower,

182

Its drawing in the grass, nor what it carves
In the notched leaves of trees, no two the same.

Ohebiel.
Here comes Akadiel. Kneel.

Phun-Abiriel.
            I worship not.
I sink into the dark.

Ohebiel.
            Alas! I follow.

AKADIEL TO NEWLY-CREATED MAN [1]
(Transl. by G. M. Gathorne-Hardy.)

MORTAL, awake! The loyal sun
Rouses thee on thy regal throne,
  In thy hall of pride,
  Ceiled with the skies,
Where ruby columns of morning rise,
And the coral arches of eventide.
  With thunder it quivers,
  With lightning is bright,
  That terrible sight
  Thy soul but delivers
  To joy sublime:
  Unmoved thou tellest
Of a temple where now thou dwellest,
With torchlight filled and the cymbals' chime.

[1] From Mennesket ("Man"), 1845. Akadiel is the first created and furthest perfected of spirits, named Messiah in "Creation," 1830.

In the calm blue depths of the vault on high,
Eternally clear o'er the clouds extending,
See thou thy Father's solemn eye,
Mortal, ever above thee bending.
Love earth as thy mother tenderly,
God made thee, but she has dreamed of thee;
   In her brute creation
See thou her lap with its blessings stored,
   In her vegetation
Her dear breast's milk, for thy food outpoured,
Yea, in the volcano there upstanding
From the hillside soft with its billows of sward
See fire, thy strongest minister, wending
In humble homage to meet his Lord.
From thyself and from all things else deduce
That move about thee in life's gay hues,—
   From high Heaven, cumbered
   With worlds unnumbered,
   From creatures that move or creep
   In the deepest deep,—
   God's power.
For the soul that the brain's white folds conceal
Let the eye interpret, the mouth reveal;
   In a choir three-fold
By the soul ecstatic, the joyous tongue
And the eye that sparkles the word be sung,
   In perception's hour,
   God's might behold!

From birds in cloud and grove
Learn thou thy solemn chant,—

"Praise be to God above,
Who joy to all doth grant,
Honour and joy to me!"
Forget not, dust thou art,
Forget not, more than dust thou art;
That the suns are the road to thy heavenly chamber,
   That in Space afar
   Each twinkling star
Is a leaf that waves o'er thy home apart
   Remember.

Mount then thy throne,
Lord whom all creatures own:
   The eagle on high
From thine arm may not fly;
No whale in depths of sea
   May hide from thee;
Well may he watch thee stand
In power upon the strand;
The lion fleet and the tiger bright
The eye of a man shall turn to flight.

   The brute restrain:
Govern thyself, the first of them all:
   To soothe, not appal,
This be thy wisdom and might:
   Lovely thy reign,
Closely with clustering blossoms bedight:
Still by thy heart before thy thought
   The truth be sought:
Be thy reason with feeling fraught,

As the sun who hides him in wreathing cloud,
Mixes his rays with the rainbow's shroud,
Nor alway with noonday force consumes,
But grants dawn dews and the eve perfumes.
  Then wide be thy sway
O'er all that is moulded or coloured in clay.
Be the new-made world's significance,
Of God's word on earth the soul and sense,
  God's speech to Himself addressed,
Inscribed in stars, that intone,
  From zone unto zone,
To the deep of the deep expressed.

AKADIEL AT THE CRUCIFIXION [1]
(Transl. by G. M. Gathorne-Hardy.)

THE patchwork cloak of the human soul,
The net of veins which immesh the whole,
  Their flickering flames infuse—
  Their burning riot of hues—
  In the soul's clear vision, and change
  It again into fancies strange.
But hereafter the soul shall achieve decision
  Twixt truth and vision,
  Shall sift the false from its hopes,
And light the shades where Religion gropes
  For that which finds expression
  So strange in Faith's confession;—
  Faith which protests

[1] From Mennesket ("Man"), 1845.

That the sweet mystery of atonement rests
In the small rose drops of the Saviour's blood,
Whose purple glows from the cross's wood
As the veil of blossom the thorn invests.
    There man shall find
    That atonement lies
    In his soul confined;
    In contrition's sighs
The whole sad story of Jesus' woe
Complete in his inmost being know.
Each fight for good that his heart maintains
Is Jesus' mother in travail pains;
Each thought of virtue his mind sets free
A Saviour born in penury;
    All good o'erborne
A Saviour mocked with a crown of thorn;
An altar of triumph each vice repressed;
But a Saviour's self is the sin bewailed
    By the contrite breast,
With shining tears to his soul fast nailed.
In tears the penitent sheds his guilt
As Jesus His pains with His blood that's spilt;
But the soul of humanity flames in might,
It braces its will and its wings for flight,
And remorse shall sink like a lifeless thing
Behind that effort, that beating wing.
    Then, when it shall see
That remorse endures not eternally,
When the soul of man in perception rises
To the height where, weeping, it realises
That the soul thus humbled is purged from sin,

That soul shall win
The Saviour's likeness, as when there rung
Farewell to earth from His dying tongue,
And the oped heaven swept Him in.

THE GROTTO AT AUCTION [1]
(Transl. by G. M. Gathorne-Hardy.)

Now shall I be of all bereft,
Stripped clean as winnowed straw:
   My house and ground,
   My horse and hound
The auctioneer is hawking round:
Yet one thing in my breast is left
Beyond the clutch of law.

A heart as steady as the clock
That ticks upon my wall:
   Its depths confine
   A cordial wine
To solace every grief of mine,
And help my buoyant soul to mock
What daily ills befall.

Yet once it stepped, when I was young,
Perchance too fast and far:
   I strove to hack
   A horse-leech black
Too brusquely from the peasant's back:
But 'twas myself, alas! was stung;
Festering and deep the scar.

[1] Auktion over "Grotten," 1844.

And whether there be truth in this
Or error, who can say?
  Myself, I must
  Believe and trust
That black and baneful worm was just
The cell where, like a chrysalis,
My evil genius lay.[1]

Light me a pipe! Already now
The auction is begun.
  Some water! Nay,
  I won't give way,
Though sometimes I can scarce be gay;
And I have just remembered how
This house with toil was won.

Perhaps some huckster in my cot
Shall make himself at home:
  Bacon and cheese,
  And things like these
Upon my favourite desk will seize;
Beer-casks will trundle in my Grot,
Brandy and gin will come.

Well, let it go! Dear little home,
I'd rather seen you fall
  In flames and smoke
  That swift outbroke,

---

[1] One of the most cryptic passages in Wergeland. The reference in this and the preceding verse is to Procurator Praëm, in attacking whom Wergeland was involved in the litigation which ruined him. Professor D. A. Seip explains the passage as meaning that after all Praëm was merely a tool in the hands of Fate.

Or blasted by a thunderstroke:
Then o'er the wrack in spring would come
Perhaps a flowery pall.

Farewell, my house! But "Brownie"[1] shall
An honest bullet end:
   His hide I've got;
   Who bids? It's not
The least bit damaged by the shot.
Don't buy my dog, though, for your call
He will not comprehend.

I'm sure to find a roof somewhere,
Will serve me for a house:
   (Four boards, one day,
   Six feet of clay,
Will stow the tallest man away),
And I will take my genius there,
My pigeons, and my spouse.

Gone is the desk I once possessed,
I write upon my knee:
   Come, dearest wife,
   We'll start the strife—
Your hand in mine—once more, of life:
But is it worth it? If you'd rest,
Then come to God with me.

Long have I gazed into the sky;
How bright the planets glow!

[1] The poet's horse.

So rich a hue
I never knew
Gleam on the lake, like harebells blue.
Help me, my wife, I know not, I,
If heaven is beckoning so.

O never shone so blue the lake,
No star was e'er so gay
  As was her glance;
  One ray did dance
To heaven, and one did me entrance . . .
Come, dear, in peace we now can take
Out in the world our way.

THE PERSONAL BEAUTY OF DEATH [1]
(Transl. by I. Grøndahl.)

My increasing indisposition had become known to
that friend of mine, who could laugh on one side of
his face, while the darkest gloom reigned on the other,
and who now came to have the notes of hope changed
into the gold of certainty.

'Thou foul and evil Death!' he cried hotly, 'Do not
come here and play the Country and Literature a
nasty trick.

'Hush! Be quiet!' I whispered. 'He is near.'

I was not then strong enough to joke with him,
though I should soon have turned the Janus face,
but on a piece of paper I wrote:

[1] Dødens personlige Skjønhed. From the autobiographical
sketches Hassel-Nødder ("Hazel Nuts"), 1845.

"The Beauty of Death.

He deserves to be run through by the long blue rapier
$\qquad$ of a deadly draught,
Who says that Death is ugly and evil.

Evil? For one year I have now been living by his
$\qquad$ mercy,
Turned away by Life, because I would suck *her* too
$\qquad$ long
And made her breasts bleed with my greediness.

Ugly? My God! Where is there a slimmer and more
$\qquad$ well-knit gentleman?
A mantle and a plumed hat, and he will out-do all the
$\qquad$ conquests of Don Juan.
Even the worms of Death are not so ugly as those that
$\quad$ just now crept over me: the false friend's fingers.
His figure has the beauty of regularity,
His face that of openness, and what can be more
$\qquad$ pleasing?
He may, however, be finer behind than in front;
But how many men are not?
A Janus face at least he has not got.

But you who have—what if even the bones in your
$\quad$ face are twisted, when you have no flesh-mask to
$\quad$ draw over them?
Then who finds your skeleton may rightly call Death
$\qquad$ ugly."

BY NIGHT IN THE HOSPITAL [1]
(Transl. by J. Bithell.)

THROUGH the big window yonder
   The full moon shines in clear.
"Are you lying there, my lover,
   Paler than I am here?

I have passed by your cottage;
   On the hearth not an ember glows;
On the wall the clock is silent,
   Dead in the window the rose.

I am going to the stars' garden.
   Cool dew there I will catch up,
And bring it for your fever
   In my horn's silver cup.

I am going to the far mountains
   That the flowers of eternity star,
Whose golden cups with nectar,
   Life's honey, laden are.

To the realm of dreams I am going;
   I will catch in my gossamer net
The loveliest pair, and with fans they
   Shall waft from your forehead the sweat.

In twenty-four hours from this minute,
   Say between one and two,
Again you may expect me
   With health and rest for you."

[1] Paa Hospitalet, om Natten. April 1845.

Now the moon with her panacea
    Has saved her poet's dreams—
Miracles are happening
    In the hospital, it seems.

Thus honours are shared as they should be,
    In the world we are living in.
He calls himself the bear's hunter,
    Who only buys its skin.

SECOND NIGHT IN THE HOSPITAL [1]
(Transl. by J. Bithell.)

THE tale I am going to tell you
    The learned will deride.
Such folks in the moon the moon see
    And nothing at all beside.

The face of a nun from Heaven
    The sick man sees, I vow;
A heavenly sister of mercy
    Is visiting him now.

Precisely as it was promised,
    The moon has passed to-night.
She brought me a golden basket,
    Heaped with roses white.

She cast them in at the window;
    They were scattered on floor and bed.
Their stalks like dewdrops glittered,
    Each like a silver thread.

[1] Anden Nat paa Hospitalet. April 1845.

So pure the roses glistened,
　My hand on the counterpane,
My white hand! was black beside them,
　As though in the grave it had lain.

My nun from Heaven whispered:
　"As these white roses shine,
Beauty's self, the ideal,
　Is clothed, and spirits divine.

This colour you shall choose now,
　With a knight's hardihood;
For these my faint, white roses
　Drink the red roses' blood.

On your lips and cheeks the white roses
　Are quenching the red roses fast.
When you are white as my roses,
　Your pain shall rest at last."

A POSSIBLE CONFUSION [1]
(Transl. by J. Bithell.)

You can keep your moon, you poets!
　With its white face woe-begone.
My moon is old Mother Saether,[2]
　With her snow-white kerchief on.

In the hospital here I have seen her,
　As up in bed I sat.
She came every night through the gateway,
　In the shape and form of a cat.

[1] Mulig Forvexling. April 1845.
[2] Henrik Ibsen lodged in the "wise woman" Mor Sæther's house, when he came to Christiania as a young man in 1850.

Scratched at his ear the porter:
"That was a wonderful puss!"
In a building full of moggies
Of cats they make a fuss.

But when she came under my window,
Straightway the cat changed her shape.
There stood a dainty old madam,
Complete in cap and cape.

A long time she stood at the window,
And stared in like the moon.—
My eyes dimmed by fever
Will be confusing them soon.

She is coming near, she is coming,
Still as the moon and as pale.
Who is sitting there? Only wildly
Can I tell the rest of my tale.

The evening star does not glitter,
Nor Mars' cornelian,
Like the drops of healing liquid
From the sybil's flask that ran.

Like phosphorus she sat there,
In a night-dress snow-white;
But the phial shone beside it
Like fire by the tree of light.

There she sat like an owl from Lapland,
The white one with golden gaze;
But the phial shone beside it,
Keen as a glacier's rays.

Nectar I quaff from a beaker,
  That is a primrose flower,
To the honour of old Mother Saether,
  And to her phial's power.

Three were the drops I tasted—
  And know it by these signs,
In the three minutes' health they gave me
  I wrote these rhymèd lines.

TO SPRING [1]
(Transl. by I. Grøndahl.)

O Spring! Spring! Save me!
No one has loved thee more dearly than I.

Thy first grass to me is worth more than emeralds.
I call thy anemones the pride of the year,
Altho' I know that the roses are coming.

Often did they, fiery, stretch out after me.
It was like being loved by princesses,
But I fled: Anemone, Spring's daughter had my troth.

Oh witness, Anemone, before whom I have fervently
                        knelt.
Witness, contemned Dandelion and Colt's-foot,
That I have valued you more than gold, because you
                        are Spring's children.

Til Foraaret. May 1845.

Witness, Swallow! that I made ready for thee
As for a long-lost child home again returned,—
Thou wast the messenger of Spring!

Seek the Lord of these clouds and pray
That they may no longer throw darts into my breast
From out of their cold, blue openings.

Witness, Old Tree! whom I have worshipped like a
                                  god,
And whose buds I have counted every spring more
                                  eagerly than pearls.

Witness, thou whom I have so often embraced,
With the reverence of a great-grandson for his great-
                                  grandfather.
Yea, how often have I not wished to be a young maple
                                  of thy deathless root,
And to blend my crown with thine!

Be my witness, Ancient One! Thou wilt be believed;
For thou art venerable as a patriarch.

Pray for me, and I will pour wine on thy roots
And heal thy scars with kisses.

Now thou art robed in thy fairest light green;
Thy leaves are rustling already.

O Spring! The old one is crying out for me, altho' he
                                  is hoarse.

He stretches his arms towards Heaven,
And the anemones, thy blue-eyed children kneel and
pray
That thou wilt save me—me who love thee so dearly.

TO MY WALLFLOWER [1]
(Transl. by I. Grøndahl.)

WALLFLOWER mine, ere thy bright hues fade,
I shall be that whereof all is made;
Ere thou hast shattered thy crown of gold,
   I shall be mould.

When 'Open the window!' I cry, from my bed,
My last look lights on thy golden head;
My soul will kiss it, as over thee
   It flieth free.

Twice do I kiss thy lips so sweet,
Thine is the first, as it is meet;
The second, dearest, my will bestows
   On my fair rose.

In bloom no more I shall it see;
So give it my greeting, when that shall be,
And say I wished on my grave should all
   Its petals fall.

Yes, say I wish that upon my breast
The rose thou gavest my kiss shall rest;
And, Wallflower, be in Death's dark porch
   Its bridal torch!

[1] Til min Gyldenlak. May 1845.

THE BEAUTIFUL FAMILY [1]
(Transl. by I. Grøndahl.)

WONDERFUL! Ah, more than wonderful!
Miracle! Oh, miracle!
Oh, that my knees could bend in adoration!

My soul has folded up its wings,
Kneeling as in a veiled chapel;
For my eyes have closed over the glory of the vision
that I have beheld.

'Do look!' I said to my wife, 'maybe I wrong the
rose-tree.
One bud may have opened last night.'

'One fully blown!' she cried, clasping her hands,
'And six half-blown around.'

'What a beautiful family!' I said.
'The full-blown one is like a mother amongst her
daughters.'

Miracle! Heavenly miracle!
In the largest rose was seated a matron, no bigger than
a humble-bee,
And clothed like the bee in golden bodice and black
skirt,
Spinning thin gossamer threads from off a pistil.

[1] Den smukke Familie. May 1845.

'Hush!' she cried. 'Open with a kiss the six half-blown
    roses, and you shall see my six eldest daughters.
We are genii, angels' hand-maids.
We are all in your mother's service.
She has sent us to prepare the clothing
Wherein your soul shall pass away from here.'

I opened, as I was told, one rose after the other.
In each of them there sat a genius, more richly clad
                            than the gold scarab.
All were working like their mother.

Their faces appeared known to me,
They seemed to belong to loved ones gone before.

'See what a glorious rose-tinged tunic you shall have!'
                            said the first.
'Don't be afraid of its being too small,' said the second.
'As soon as it comes into the open air it will widen.'

'I am washing your scarf,' said the third,
Washing some filmy golden threads in a dew-drop.

'And I! and I!' said the others as I came to them in
'Look! Look!'   [turn,

And one was preparing some attar of roses to anoint
                            the delicate feathers
Which they said the soul already wore.

One was busy making a pair of sandals, which looked
  like a couple of tiny curled leaves from the interior
  of the rose.

'With them you can tread the glowing floor of the
                    sun,' she said,
And sewed on, with an awl no bigger than the sting
                    of a gnat.

The sixth sat idle with her hands resting in her lap.
'I have done,' she said. 'Mother has already got my
                    work, so I can talk a little.
But don't you know me? I am the poor child you
                    wished were yours.'

'Look!' she chatted away. 'We are more than seven,
  we are twenty-one.' And to my astonishment I
  counted fourteen more buds.

'Only when the last one opens,' she went on,
'Do we wish that you will fly with us to Heaven,
And you shall see how large and fine we grow in our
                    flight.

In the last bud there lies only a canary-bird, no bigger
                    than a barley-corn,
And a scarlet bull-finch, no bigger than a garnet.

Your mother sends them to let you know that you
                    shall meet in Heaven
All that you have loved, even the least.
The dear little ones will fly back with us.

When the heart is lifted into glory, the innocent
    earthly things which it has loved cling to it as to
    a magnet . . .'

'Hush!' whispered the sweet babbler.
'I am betraying the secrets of Heaven's religion.

I will tell you this more, that you shall see your horse
                        if you long to.
You shall seem to lay your hand on his neck.

In a cloud valley you shall see him browsing
Carnations to the right and gilly-flowers to the left.

Would you ride him once more?
Good! Heaven has wide plains.

It will please your mother to see that you have not
                        forgotten her favourite,
Whom she has stroked so often.

She has told us that Brownie would come every day
                        to her window,
And gaze at her with his intelligent eyes
Until the kindly hand came forth.

Surely her heart will beat with joy at your ride on
                        him,
As she knows that yours rejoices when you tear up
    along one of the mountains of Thunder,
Or across one of the streams of Lightning.

Now I have spoken; now let the rose fold up,
For I need rest after my work.
This only yet: as soon as the last bud has opened,
Our work-cells will fall in, and we will hasten back to
　　　　　　　　　　　　　　　your mother
With the heavenly garment she is giving to her first-
　　　　　　　　　　　　　　　born.'